Peeking Behind the Scenes:

A deliberate path to success

Compiled by Jennifer Low

Peeking Behind the Scenes: A Deliberate Path to Success

Publisher: www.ManlPublishing.com
Editor: Jennifer Low.

Printed in Canada and USA

ISBN: 978-0-9949284-2-9
E-Book ISBN: 978-0-9949284-3-6

DISCLAIMER

Table of Contents

Gratitude…………………………………………...………....1
Foreword James MacNeil……………………………..……3
Introduction………………………………………….........7

Chapter 1   Success is 10 % Inspiration and 90 %
Perspiration
By Ahmad-Shah Duranai……………………15

Chapter 2   From Rock Bottom to Rock Solid: Beating
the Odds of Becoming Successful
By Patricia LeBlanc………………………29

Chapter 3   The Plan Starts by Taking Action
By Symona Vitali……………………….....41

Chapter 4   It's all About the Attitude
By Norman Douglas…………………………..53

Chapter 5   Self-Empowerment: That's the Secret Sauce
in the Journey to Success
By Ms. Pino……………………………….....63

Chapter 6   Blood Sweat and Success
By Dr. Lauren E. Karatanevski…………………77

Chapter 7   Success was Always There: I Just had to
Open my Eyes!
By Jennifer Low………………………….....91

Chapter8   Pattern Interrupt
By Paquita Varee Wright…………………101

Chapter 9   A Peek Behind the Scenes to my
Deliberate Path
By Arlene Pe Benito……………………113

Chapter 10   Keep Moving Forward
By Holly A. Kline………………………125

Chapter 11   Pivots
              By Jane "Trainer Jane" Warr……………........135
Chapter 12   I Am Enough
              By Holly Porter…………………………………147
Chapter 13   Roots and Wings
              By Theresia Valoczy…………………………159
Chapter 14   Dance to the Music of Your Heart
              By Agnes Kazmierczak…………………….....171
Chapter 15   Steps to Fly: 7 Steps to Transforming your
              Dream of Living Abroad into a Challenging
              and Enchanting Reality
              By Roberta Weber Calabró…………………183
Chapter 16   Stick To Your Passion
              By Lison Ouellette…………………………197
Chapter 17   Follow Your Dreams: My Life, My Way!
              By Aldona Konkol………..………………….209
Chapter 18   Resetting My Settings
              By Kedian Jimenez…………………….......221
Chapter 19   A Life Long Journey…
              By Linda P. Cousineau………………..…….233
Chapter 20   Always Stretching and Always Striving
              By Al Hillman……………….…………...……245
Chapter 21   Confessions of an Overnight Success
              By Sandi Cohen P.S…..……………………255

Conclusion ……………..…………………………….....269

Compiled by **JENNIFER LOW**

Gratitude

Before I lead you on a magical journey of success, I would like to start by thoroughly acknowledging and elevating all the people who have contributed to this book:

Agnes, Ahmad, Al, Aldona, Arlene, Holly K, Holly P, Jane, Kedian, Lauren, Linda, Lison, Martha, Norman, Paquita, Patricia, Roberta, Sandi, Symona and Theresia.

Thank you for believing in me and in my dream of inspiring others through your story and your journey. You have single handedly helped better humanity by sharing an intimate part of you. Thank you for having the courage to step forward into this journey and into this new life with me.

If you are here with me, behind this cover, it's because you are bold and brave, you are important, and you matter, and you were meant to be here in this newly formed community.

Thank you for your participation and for your dedication.
Thank you for shining your light onto others.
I appreciate you, I value you, I honour you!

Thank you James MacNeil for taking the time to contribute in opening up the stage for us to peek behind the scenes.

PEEKING BEHIND THE SCENES

Special thanks to Patricia LeBlanc who has done another excellent job with this anthology and who has been methodically leading me by the hand down this garden path. I am so grateful that you took me on as one of your co-authors back in January of 2015. I am very thankful for having been given this opportunity and to have acted on it. That first experience of truly expressing my life in words has absolutely changed it all around for me!

I am most grateful for my family whom I wake up with every day. Thank you, Joshua, for loving me and smiling at me every single day of our life together. Thank you, Anika, for shining your delicate love all over this home. I am eternally grateful for your glowing presence in my life. And thank you, Mira, for being such a great spark. You were worth waiting 38 years for!

Lastly, I am grateful for you, my reader, for without you, this book would never have been written! You have given us all the opportunity to share part of our richest fortunes with you.

Thank you!

Foreword

by James MacNeil

The Science of Success has been a healthy obsession of mine for over 30 years and sharing the best of my research has been my profession for the last 25 years. I've invested these years on stage, learning my craft, sharpening my art of selling, teaching, and coaching, and in the process, witnessing many lives I have had the privilege to positively impact. I have shared the stage with the likes of Tony Robbins, Bob Proctor, Les Brown, Sir Richard Branson and many others. I have circled the globe seven times now and have even had opportunities to work with some of the world's most powerful banks.

Success and accomplishment, to the degree I've enjoyed them, are wonderful, but the challenges are never over. In fact, my entire life story revolves around facing, managing, and overcoming the multiple challenges thrown at me. As a kid, I had some unique challenges that made me, for a lack of a better term, a giant pain in the ass. This applied to home as well as school. I was segregated by my peers and pushed through the school system by my teachers.

At 18, my family disbanded. I was functionally illiterate, and fearing homelessness on the cold streets of Toronto, Canada, I decided I was going to do it in style. So I bought a car for $500, packed everything I owned in it and drove it straight South to Florida. Shortly after I got there, someone stole my car with everything I owned in it. I thought: "Oh God, seriously!! This isn't funny anymore."

Things only started to spiral down from there: loneliness, depression, and ugly behavior set in.

And then, by the grace of God, at 20, I was subject to a spiritual awakening. As a result, I had a complete paradigm shift, which reshaped my entire life and brought me on a path of achievement, satisfaction, discovery, privilege and fulfillment.

There is no end to the challenges that are going to come. But is there any end to our capacity to face, manage, and grow through those challenges? I believe life is tough, life is unfair, and there's no free lunch, but we can make our life a treasure and a shining example if we strive persistently to realize our best possible life, as our best possible selves. I like what Jim Rohn said: "Don't wish life was easier, just wish you were better."

For me, I just want to be the man who is capable of managing the reality I face. I strive to be the man who I feel I've been "called" to be. It's just a never-ending quest of asking myself, "can I rise to the occasion, can I get back up again, can I climb out of whatever hole I find myself in to reach new heights of service and accomplishment?"

One of the benefits I have received from all of my experiences was that staying still, for me, meant death. Where other people think staying still is safe, I knew staying still would be the end for me. I had to progress to survive. I had to make something happen. I had this *leaning forward into life* mentality that was required at the beginning. Now I don't know how to turn it off no matter what I accomplish or learn or earn. I keep *leaning in* because now I want to see what I can do with this life.

If you want to peek behind the scenes and truly want to understand what makes any great life, any great achievement, any great accomplishment, you must take a look at the complexity of the millions of moments that made up that accomplishment. The greatness lies in all those moments of patience, of persistence, of transition, of tragedy and of triumph, and the millions of little decisions and choices.

Peeking Behind The Scenes: a deliberate path to success is raw and real. These are real people recounting their story through the revelation of their challenges and by exposing their 'before and after' facet. The most challenging point in their life also illustrates a significant turning point to them.

PEEKING BEHIND THE SCENES

Something that made them come up with that one big decision that slingshotted them in the right direction. These are everyday people, ordinary people, who have courageously made the right choices for themselves and have, by this process, changed the course of their life forever.

Treat this book as a treasure hunt! It is a valuable read, because of the many varied stories which allow for the many different views of success. From divorce come back, illness, near-death situation, to leaving the corporate world, beating the odds, surmounting mountains of debt, and pursuing your dream with conviction, deliberately putting yourself through uncomfortable situations just to go beyond what is known, and to see what lies on the other side. I trust your breakthrough insights and words of encouragement are between these covers.

These people will inspire you to take action in your own life, to follow your heart, to know it is possible, because many made it happen without knowing what the outcome would be.

They made it happen! And so can you.

Introduction

Every journey starts with a single step. That initial step can sometimes even be an idea that you voice 'in passing'. And Poof! The path starts to appear. This is where you released it out of you. It's where you let the Universe hear what your wishes and desires are, and reveal to you, in that moment, what your true life direction is. Voicing a message like this out loud may even come as a surprise to yourself! Such as this book…

Let me explain.

On day 2 of 2016, I was on a call with a friend of mine. We were planning our work year out loud to each other when she announced to me that this year, it was my turn to compile my own anthology. Yes, she said that to me as a statement.

I had recently participated in a co-authored book with her and was published for the first time in the fall of 2015. It was an exciting moment of my life. I had had the privilege of being privy to the entire project, as I had signed up towards its very beginning and implicated myself wholeheartedly to this cause all the way through to its release in print. This book flourished before my eyes. I was so proud to present it to the world.

As I held my first copy of *Manifesting A New Life* in my hands, I toyed with the idea of having my own name on a book.

PEEKING BEHIND THE SCENES

Feeling my path was still a long way's away, I dropped that thought almost as quickly as it had arrived. Yet on that 2nd day of the New Year, when asked what the title of this anthology would be, should I be writing it this year, the words effortlessly flowed off my tongue: "Peeking Behind The Scenes: a deliberate path to success". As soon as I had said it I found myself dumbfounded. I knew its title, its subtitle, what this book would look like, and what it would be about in its entirety. Had I actually thought about it long enough that my subconscious had taken over or was it so divinely 'meant to be' that a Spirit had borrowed my breath?

Regardless of how or why it came about, this book was naturally starting its incubation period.

Allow me to bring you back in time and reveal to you how this concept of success originally came to the forefront of my life.

In the summer of 2008, my life was subject to a drastic change of direction. That July, I had gone to Spain with the kids for two weeks. Three days prior to our return to Canada, I received an email from my then-husband stating that he had been to see a lawyer in my absence. I couldn't sleep that night. I was literally consumed with stress and anxiety. I lay in bed staring at the semi-darkened walls, listening to the sound of my young daughter's rhythmic breathing, while she slept peacefully beside me. My adult life had always been about my kids. They were my purpose, my career, my sole occupation.

For 15 years, I had become a voluntary financial dependent. I had no assets of my own, no disposable cash, no family to back me up in the city I currently lived in, and I did not know what I was going 'home' to. All I knew is that I had return flights, that I couldn't let the kids in on this, that I had to be the pillar they expected me to be, and that life was about to take a new turn.

And boy did life ever change!

The financial stress that followed the trip to Spain was something I vowed never to experience again. Slowly, gradually, progressively, my drive to strive, to grow, and ultimately to triumph in monetary success became my obsession. I studied, I observed, I applied, and I made a conscious choice to get involved with the right communities.

So many of us strive for success. We want to climb that mountain bravely and be the best. Sometimes it's to prove something to ourselves, sometimes it's to prove something to others, sometimes it's simply because we want the monetary rewards to provide more for ourselves and for our family, …and sometimes it's just because we want to stretch to be the very best we can be and find true purpose in our reason for existing!

PEEKING BEHIND THE SCENES

In the eyes and in the minds of most people, success is often associated with money. It was for me too… This is because even though people equate the two terms (that of money and success) as being synonymous with each other, what truly feeds this formula is that one is the result of the other. This is part of the very first universal law of life: the law of Cause and Effect.

Those of us who have touched, smelled, seen, and felt success know this: that success has a price. Sometimes it comes as a singular sacrifice, or as many layered sacrifices. Sometimes that price comes in brick walls. That's the test to find out how badly you really want it, exposing to you the challenge of whether you are willing to do whatever it takes to get to your goal and to your success. When the Universe sees how dedicated you truly are, in due time, you will be rewarded many times over.

What starts with a simple request of ourselves, often turns out to be the iceberg of what truly lies under the surface to one's life purpose. It is the awakening of our true force that eventually becomes the fuel of our success.

Success has a very personal definition to each and every one of us. To some, success means achievement. To others, it means to live another day. The common thread, though, is that success takes time. It takes practice. It takes devotion and dedication. Success has that unknown factor that is tied to the fear of failure, leaving us at times to walk only in Faith. Success calls us into action. It causes us to push our boundaries beyond what we initially may have conceived as possible.

According to Napoleon Hill, Thomas Edison always applied what he had observed in Nature to his world of expansion and innovation.

I'd like to take this a step further for a moment and fast forward to current times. I invite you to look at the incredible similarities between the principles of our modern space travel and that of the trajectory of success.

Let's start with the physics of it. We live in a world enveloped in a multitude of atmospheric layers that keep us safe. The only way for us to get into space is by generating a huge propulsion out of our safety zone. For the Shuttle to lift off, it needs to carry its own fuel cylinder as well as two rocket boosters to create enough momentum to get it off the pad and out of this atmosphere. Yet once it has gone past that safety zone, that atmospheric barrier, it needs virtually no more energy to travel. It simply floats, effortlessly!

How many times have we seen success as the necessity to get out of one's comfort zone, and to give it so much dedication and devotion, so much of our personal energy, to create that momentum that we need to propel ourselves forward into 'progress'? Yet once all the momentum is established, success is inevitable because of critical mass. Then it is followed by what seems to be an easy glide period.

Continuing with this example, let's look at it from a historic point of view and illustrate time perspective. It was during a 1961 speech delivered by John F. Kennedy that this concept of space travel was first presented to the people. The president at the time made what many thought was an extravagant promise: a man on the moon before the end of the decade. Sure enough, on July 20th 1969, a human set foot on the moon.

Big endeavours take time even though we would rather they didn't. It is important to keep a perspective on our own success in this way too. Celebrate each small step. Taste the journey.

It's also worth noting that at the time of his announcement, the president knew he was not going to do this alone. He put people in charge of assembling the best and most qualified team for this project. Solo-preneurship had no place in this. It was all about quality team building. The Roman Empire wasn't mighty on a two-person committee. Wars were never fought with just one soldier in each camp. Real strength only comes in numbers! Victory happens when a group of people can work towards a worthy cause as well as towards a common goal.

I now have the pleasure of introducing you to MY team: twenty one authors, sharing their own journey to success, and what it meant for them to have chosen entrepreneurship. Our common goal is to expose the challenges, and the triumphs that we went through, as well as our mindset over the course of our journey. Our worthy cause through this book is to encourage you to take that first step to your greatness. Our purpose is to inspire you to keep moving forward if you have already taken that step, or if you are now experiencing the bitter sweetness of being the person who is building a true asset. We are here to give you hope that good does come out of this. Success is about the mastery of patience, of persistence, of consistency and of dedication.

The concept of **Peeking Behind The Scenes** is about digging deep below the surface of what you may initially see and may have made judgment upon. It's about revealing to you the true grit, what it took to "get there", and to understand the work, the ethics, the application of the universal success principles, and the rigorous self-discipline we have had to impose on ourselves.

It takes time and yes, it does pay off.

PEEKING BEHIND THE SCENES

Work smarter, not harder.
Stay in action to keep traction.
Trust in divine timing.

Welcome to the world of **Peeking Behind The Scenes**!

Ahmad-Shah Duranai

Ahmad-Shah Duranai is the Author of the book THE LEADERSHIP ZONE and AN OUTSIDE-THE-BOX LOOK AT AFGHANISTAN.

Ahmad has over 30 years experience working with international design firms as Architect and Project Manager on major and iconic projects in North America and the Middle East. He is a member of OAA and affiliate member of ICF.

He is CEO and Head Coach at Duranet Enterprises Inc. providing Coaching and Training Programs in leadership and communications.

Ahmad is the 2013 recipient of the Lieutenant Governor of Ontario Award and Medal in Humanities / Social Justice & For Exceptional Services rendered to the Community.

He can be contacted at:

Tel: + 1 647 222 6772

Email: ahmad@duranet.ca

Web: http://www.duranet.ca/

Chapter 1

Success is 10 % Inspiration and 90 % Perspiration

By Ahmad-Shah Duranai

When I was a student in the American University of Beirut in Lebanon, studying architecture, there was a saying that floated around which went like this: "great design is 10 % inspiration and 90 % perspiration." As the years went by and I observed the way students studied and worked, including myself, on their design projects, I became one hundred percent convinced of the truth and validity of that statement.

I noticed that students who scored high were not those who got inspired design concepts but those who spent 24, 36 or 48 hours of non-stop work on preparing presentation boards for the defense of their designs in front of a jury of professors.
Those long hours were necessary to take the inspired concepts and develop them into presentable, clear and mature project ideas. Many years later when I transitioned from Architecture into Success coaching, and as I studied the ecology and morphology of success, I observed the patterns of the success of those who have made it (including my own), and the idea

of 10/90 came strikingly back into the forefront of my thinking. Success is generally the result of 10 % inspiration and 90 % perspiration – Hence the title of the chapter. I will come to this statement later, but let's first agree on the meaning and definition of SUCCESS.

What is Success?

If we were to ask a hundred people to write down in one or two sentences what success means to them, we would for sure find 100 different statements. And that is when and where the confusion starts. People usually don't agree on a common definition.

At the start of my Success 101™ Seminars, we distribute a form asking participants to write in one or two sentences what success means to them in various pathways such as career, relationships, finances, health, etc. We collect the forms and keep them for the duration of the program. Over the years we have discovered that each person has his / her own definition of success and the information on each form is different. At the end of 4 weekly sessions, when the program is finished we distribute the blank form again and ask them to write afresh what success means to them after completing the program. We then give them the forms they filled at the start of the program to compare if there is any difference. Usually, the graduates who pay a lot of attention and do all the assignments see a much bigger difference between their original writing and the new one. We use this as a measure of assessing the collective success of the program.

There is very little agreement even at the level of masters in the personal development industry on a common definition of SUCCESS. Among the numerous definitions, I have selected two that resonate with me. One definition comes from the traditional literature that goes back to Earl Nightingale and Napoleon Hill. According to them "Success is the progressive realization of a worthy goal or ideal."

The other definition is according to Meir Ezra who states that "Success is the sum total of all validated improvements." I want you (the reader) to choose the one that resonates best with your paradigms. In all cases, success is a change, a positive change in a person's current status.

How to Achieve Success?

There is a general misconception among many people that success is the destiny of only a select group of people who are naturally talented and have God given gifts that are embedded in their genes. This myth has become widespread, because most literature on success and successful people focuses on the final outcome of their efforts. It rarely goes into detail of all the hard work and the numerous failures that the so-called "successful" people go through before they are recognized as successful.

Based on my observation and personal experience, I find that every success story is preceded by many failures. The reason that we do not hear about the hard work and the numerous failures is that most failures are not sensational and do not create any hype. There are generally three types of failures: Failures that are catastrophic in nature.

Failures that become the lot of those who after a few attempts give up their dreams and let all their efforts go to waste. Failures that become "lessons learned" by people who are driven by compelling visions and who are persistent, committed and don't give up easily.

Of the three types only the first type of failures get media attention and are reported. Since they are not followed by any kind of success, they are presented without any connection to success. The media ignores the other two types of failures. Failures also do not inspire people either to buy or to role model so they are ignored on the stage as well, except as a counterpoint to emphasize success.

It is usually the third type of failure that eventually leads to Success as defined earlier. Before I go in to my personal story, here are a few success examples of famous celebrities and industry leaders to clarify the point I am making: Thomas Edison and the invention of the incandescent lamp – while the success of the incandescent lamp had tremendous impact in the lives of people all over the world, he failed thousands of times in his experiment and did not give up. That is how he succeeded.

Colonel Sanders' recipe for Kentucky Fried Chicken – he is said to have tried to use his recipe with many food outlets, but failed until he finally used it in his own gas station in Corbin, Kentucky from where he started his franchise chain.

Jack Canfield and Mark Victor Hansen tried 144 publishers to publish their Chicken Soup for the Soul book series without any success. They too did not give up and eventually managed to find a publisher.

Thousands of other success stories have followed similar patterns of numerous failures before showing up like the tip of an iceberg.

My personal Story

Based on my accomplishments, I consider myself a success story. I was born in a small village in Paktia, a province of Afghanistan, in a village that is 120 km south of Kabul, but at least 120 years behind it in cultural and economic development. To this day, people in the area do not have running water or electricity in their homes. They do not have access to healthcare, proper educational facilities or any other infrastructure services that we take for granted here in Canada. Only recently has the wireless telephone system reached the villages that use solar energy to charge the devices.

People have a subsistence level of life, and when I was a child, there was one school, and it took us more than an hour of walking to reach it. So in those initial and formative years, success for me was 10% BLESSING and 90% STRESSING...
The BLESSING was that my parents enrolled me in school instead of making me work with them full time at home and on the farm, like most other children were doing. The STRESSING came from the fact that in addition to attending the school and doing the assignments, I had to help my parents by either grazing the animals after school or working in the Inn that my father and his cousins owned in the village bazaar. So during the daylight hours, I was either in school or outside the house grazing our domestic animals. We had cows that provided milk, oxen used for plowing the land and donkeys for carrying stuff, and every year we would raise a ram as a source of dry meat for the long winters.

There was no time to do school assignments during the day. In the evenings after dinner I would sit in the front of a primitive homemade kerosene lamp to do my homework. My father would make sure I finished the homework before I could go to sleep. In addition to all of this, I was raised as a Muslim and had to allocate time for the daily obligatory prayers. Obligatory prayers is the 2nd of the five pillars of Islam and Muslims are required to pray five times every day at assigned times – before sunrise (Fajr), noon time (Zohor), before sunset (Asr), immediately after sunset (Maghreb) and later in the evening before sleeping (Isha).

It was really tough to do all those things as a daily routine: to walk more than two hours to and from school, spend time in school and focus on the lessons to learn something, graze livestock when back at home, do the homework in front of the dim light of a kerosene lamp and also to make sure I didn't miss the prayers. But all in all, I learned tremendously from my experience in those early formative years and I learned several lessons that have guided me throughout my life and have helped me in achieving so much to be grateful for. Here are the most important ones:

Role Model

I was lucky to have older brothers who had gone through a similar routine. So I relied on their experience and improved on it. This has been a big lesson that has helped me over the years. I have used role models and have followed their steps in most endeavours and tasks that I have undertaken. It has helped me in university, in the workplace and in business. Role models help in shortening the path and the learning curve.

Self-discipline

I learned how to juggle all the various tasks I had to do and do them properly; I had to learn how to allocate time to each. In those early days, I learned that anything, which I did not do properly, had penal consequences. Flagellation was common in the school system and whenever we did not learn the lessons or missed classes or did not do the homework, we would be punished physically, and for me that was both painful and scary. To avoid it I had to learn both discipline and accountability so that I would not be subjected to it as often as some others were. Similarly, if I did not take good care of the animals, I would face disciplinary action from my parents. To avoid the customary discipline from the parents and teachers, I learned how to discipline myself. The self-discipline I learned at that time has helped me in all my life especially when I was in high school, university, and in the workplace and when I was living away from home after the age of 12 and had no family support on a daily, weekly or monthly basis.

PEEKING BEHIND THE SCENES

Accountability

In my experience, Accountability and Self-discipline go together and complement each other. In addition to keeping myself accountable to avoid the punishment, I used my elder brother to keep me in line and remind me how to take care of things if I lapsed into procrastination in any area. When I lived in the dormitory and away from home, I used my friends to keep me accountable for the things I had to do.

When I was writing my last book- *THE LEADERSHIP ZONE: Lessons from the Front Lines*, I went through a short period of writer's block and procrastination. Knowing how important a role accountability had played in my previous successes, I asked a friend who is a professional coach, to be my Accountability Coach. It was with her accountability skills that I successfully completed that book which has since changed the lives of many people.

Learn How the System Works

One of the things that I also learned early in life and had a major impact on my outcomes is to find out how the system works and to be deliberate about it. I would say learning this secret has helped me on many occasions not only to reduce pain, hard work, and failure but also to ensure success. For example in high school and university, I learned the secrets of

24

how to study effectively and how to score high in tests and exams, how to prepare for multiple-choice questions and how to prepare for essay type exams. I discovered that the best way to learn a topic is to teach it so I would do that with my close friends when we did our homework and assignments together.

In the workplace, where client relations are very important, I would find out how the client organization operates, how is the performance of the client reps evaluated in their organization, and how I could help them to do good in that, and shine.

I learned the skill sets associated with the above lessons and principles. They have helped me to succeed in most of my accomplishments.

They helped me in high school to excel academically and get a full scholarship to study abroad in a high standard elite university.

They helped me succeed and excel in university which was located away from home in a completely different cultural and social environment.

They helped me when in 1985 I immigrated to Canada (yet another completely different cultural and social environment) and settled successfully, sponsored my family from a refugee camp to join me, got married, raised two handsome and successful children and have had a rewarding career.

They helped me when I managed teams of designers and creative talent to create iconic pieces of architecture in Canada and the Middle East.

They helped me when I transitioned to become The Leadership and Communications Coach and started Duranet Enterprises Inc. and when I designed and created my cutting edge seminars and workshops – Success 101™, Success Unlimited™ and Leadership DARE™.

They helped me when I authored a great book on Leadership and was able to interview leaders such as Peter Aceto, and thought leaders such as Stephen M. R. Covey and others as part of my research. A book that according to Gerry Robert, Best Selling Author of the Millionaire Mindset, is " *indeed a roadmap for life on purpose and a holistic manual on leadership. I can easily visualize a copy of it on the shelves of leaders, executives, managers, business owners and entrepreneurs everywhere.*"

They helped me to be invited and travel to faraway places and share my skills and knowledge with people in international organizations.

These principles and the skills associated with them are definitely not in my DNA. They are learnable skills, and everyone can adapt them. I may have been exposed to and learned them in the harsh realities of Afghanistan, but they can be learned anywhere, anytime and at any age.

They have helped me, and perhaps they can help you too if you are willing to put up with perspiration and hard work, to master these skills and live by these principles.

PEEKING BEHIND THE SCENES

Patricia LeBlanc

Patricia LeBlanc is a Dream Maker. She empowers Spiritual Female Entrepreneurs to get out of their own way so that they can create the life and business that they desire. Patricia helps her clients get clear on what they want, release their money blocks and charge what they are truly worth.

Patricia is an Award winning Author, International Speaker and Trainer, Manifesting and Business Strategist as well as a Master Energy Healer and Teacher.

Let Patricia help you like she has helped thousands before you. Apply for your free consultation by visiting www.YourAbundanceCoach.com/Consultation

You can contact Patricia by Email: info@patricialeblanc.ca

Chapter 2

From Rock Bottom to Rock Solid: Beating the Odds of Becoming Successful

By Patricia LeBlanc

Successful people are not born successful. Most successful people actually have everything going against them, but are so determined to make it to the top of their field that they do just that. They have faith that they will make it happen. They choose to jump in fully and do whatever it takes to reach their dreams and goals. They never quit. They may take a step back to re-evaluate, and they keep moving forward.

Let me start by sharing with you a part of my journey starting with one of my major turning points.

In 2004, I was diagnosed with a major clinical depression that followed several minor ones. I am genetically prone to them. I even had suicidal thoughts. This was one of my worst moments and at the same time, one of my greatest blessings. It took me a long time to come out of it. I was lost and had no care in the world. I did not know who I was anymore as I had been listening to everyone else.

Growing up I had huge dreams. I was going to be a very successful entrepreneur and was going to change the world. Somehow I got lost along the way. I listened to what others wanted for me. I took the safe route because it was expected of me. I went the corporate route instead of starting my own business. As a child, I was a real introvert and would give away my power and my voice by letting certain people speak on my behalf.

One day I woke up thinking: "What am I doing with my life? What happened with my childhood dreams?" That morning was the start of discovering who I was and even more importantly the self-discovery of what my life purpose was. It was a long process as not only did I need to find out who I was, I also needed to get my power and my voice back and learn what my gifts were. Since I am multi-gifted, it was a real struggle for me. It was hard for me to blend these gifts together. In fact when I stopped resisting and started using all of my gifts that is when business started to grow with ease and grace.

In 2012, I was in a car accident. My friend and I were very lucky to have survived it. This was a very big pivotal point for me. I finally fully woke up. I realized this was my wake up call from the Universe and if I did not do anything for myself, the next time I would not survive. It was as simple as that! I could not let that happen as I knew I was meant to play big and transform and inspire millions of people. I was meant to make the world a better place.

That car accident was my BIG wake up call. From that moment on, I did whatever it took to go after my dreams. I started to believe that it was possible for me to achieve my childhood dreams and goals.

I started taking a multitude of courses. I got certified in several modalities such as a Law of Attraction Advanced Practitioner, Master Life Coach, and Integrated Energy Healing Master Instructor.

I also knew my major weaknesses in business were in the areas of sales, marketing, social media and building relationships. I invested a lot of money, energy and time to learn and master these skills. I am by far no expert, but I know enough now to grow my business and to be confident in those areas.

A lot of people think that in 2014 I woke up and became an overnight success. You see, in 2014, I co-wrote 5 International Best Selling Books of which one of them became a #1 International Best Seller. In reality, people could not have been further from the truth. My mindset was so messed up. I would self-sabotage and hide. I was close to being completely broke. In fact, it took me approximately 12 years to get from where I was to where I currently am. My success did not come without its own share of struggles. I am now truly abundant in all areas of my life.

When I first started my business, I would focus more on coaching as this was one of my gifts. Everyone was telling me that I needed to only focus on coaching. I suppressed the intuitive and energy healing side of me. This brought me out of alignment, I struggled a lot and was not successful. I was giving everything away for free. I then did a 180 degree shift, stopped coaching altogether and started doing only energy healing work. This worked better, but I was still out of alignment.

I would also listen to what every single successful person would tell me to do in my business. I had 6 and 7 figure business owners telling me to do this and to do that. Guess what? None of it worked, as it was not in alignment with me.

Late in 2015, I realized that I was meant to use ALL of my gifts. I now do Abundance Attraction strategy consultation, energy healing, write, and publish books. I am in alignment with myself and with my life purpose, and my business is flourishing. Now, when someone gives me advice, I stop to see if it resonates with me and my business. If it is not in alignment, then I do not take it on.

PEEKING BEHIND THE SCENES

In 2014, I started working on what would become my International Best Selling Book Series: *Manifesting a New Life*. Book #1 was a 15 month journey that was supposed to take only 4 to 5 months tops. Boy, what a journey that was. I was facing challenges in all areas of my life. In June 2015, I almost threw in the towel. I was so ready to quit and go back into the corporate world. That was how bad I was being tested. I was fed up. Luckily for me, I stood my ground and did not give up. This is also when I let go of the outcome and just let the Universe guide me. It was the best thing I did as the book turned out better than what I could ever have imagined. *Manifesting a New Life: Money, Love, Health and Everything in Between*, which is book #1, was a life changer for me. It allowed me to grow, become confident, and gain perspective on where I was supposed to go next in my business and in my life. It also became an International Best Seller within several hours of launching, and we reached #2 in the dream category between *Think and Grow Rich* and *Chicken Soup for The Soul: Dreams and Premonitions*.

Book #2, *Manifesting a New Life: Your Magical Guide to Attracting the life that you want*, was a much easier journey and was even more rewarding. I got to enjoy the ride a lot more. If I would have quit, I would not have created 40 International Best Selling Authors, I would not have created an International Best Selling book series, nor would I have changed the lives of other people including my own. I am so grateful that I did whatever it took and did not give up. I could not imagine my life without it.

When I was young, I always knew that I would be very successful and would make a difference in the world. I just never knew what it was going to be or what it was going to look like. Now that I know what my life purpose is, I am so glad that I pushed through and did whatever it took after my major depression to discover who I was and what my purpose was. I am so grateful that I never quit as I came so close at least a thousand times. It was a real struggle for me to connect the dots. I am so grateful now that I did the hard work. All the sacrifices were worth it. Keep at it until you succeed. I am so blessed that I had my Dad as a role model! My Dad has been chronically ill most of his adult life. I can count on one hand how often my dad complained about being in pain. I can tell you most people would have given up years ago. He is mentally very strong. I am grateful that I got this quality from him.

I am now a Leading Law of Attraction and Abundance Attraction Expert, a Master Energy Healer and Teacher, International Speaker, and Trainer and 2 time #1 Best Selling Author, Compiler, and Publisher as well as a 13 time International Bestselling Author. I get asked all the time to appear on media and to be part of various summits, which some have guest experts such as my mentor Dr. Joe Vitale from the Secret. I have accomplished more in the last 2 years than I have in my entire lifetime. Even more importantly, I am making my dreams come true while being 1000% true to myself.

Over the years I have studied successful people, and they all use these success principles. Let me share with you my top 10 tips on how I became successful. Take what works for you and make it your own.

Here are my top 10 success tips:

Take 100% responsibility for the state of your life

Successful people know that they are 100% responsible for the state of their life. Victims blame others 100% of the time. So make a conscious decision today to start by taking responsibility for 100% of the things that happen to you. Look at how you attracted-them into your life and make applicable changes. Look at what life lessons you need to learn. When I started taking 100% responsibility for my life, my results changed. This is not an easy one to master especially if you have a victim mindset. Start with where you are as you are perfectly in the right place, and work on getting better at taking 100% responsibility.

Do not share your dreams with the naysayers

I have learned the hard way to not share my dreams with people who do not support me. A lot of times, people will try to discourage you not because they mean to, but because they do not believe that it is possible for them. They do not want you to fail. Or they may be jealous because you have the guts to go after your dream

Surround yourself with positive, uplifting people

It is very important to surround yourself with successful, positive and uplifting people. This will help you to keep going especially when fear kicks in. I do an inventory of the people in my life on a regular basis. If you are not positive and you do not inspire me to be a better person, you get released from my life. This is very important, because if you spend time with people who are negative and who pull you down, your energy will get drained.

Believe in yourself no matter what

It is very important that you believe in yourself no matter what! If you do not believe in yourself, it will make it hard for you to succeed. Make certain that you have a few people who believe in you and when you stop believing in yourself, reach out to them. I have been very fortunate to have several people who believed in me and would encourage me when I was ready to quit everything. When you believe in yourself, anything is possible. Especially during the challenging times.

Get out of your own way

If you want to be successful, you will need to get out of your comfort zone. Trust me on this one. Growing up, I was the empathic introverted kid. I hated doing any kind of public speaking and look at me now: I am an international speaker and trainer. I do things every day that stretch me out of my comfort zone.

Find a mentor/coach

It is important to find a mentor, someone who has accomplished what you want to. This will help save you a lot of time, hard work, energy and even money. I wish that I would have taken this advice early on instead of trying to do everything myself. I am so blessed that I have people whom I trust and value and who want only the best for me. I now reach out to them when I am stuck or need a sounding board.

Know what you want

It is very important if you want to be successful that you know exactly what it is that you want. If you are not crystal clear, not only don't you have any direction, but you also cannot attract it into your life. It is as simple as that.

Take action

It is very important that you take some sort of action every single day towards your goals and dreams. When the opportunities, ideas, and/or people come to you, you need to act on it!!! If you do not, then you will not achieve your goal/dream. The Universe wants to give you what you want, but it takes action on your part.

Be grateful for everything that you have

It is important that you are grateful for everything that you have. Find the blessings in every life lesson. I start my day by saying "THANK YOU Universe for giving me the gift of another day and for every gift that is on its way to me." I also write in my gratitude journal and let me tell you when I do not do this regularly, my day is a struggle and it pulls me away from being successful.

Jump in 100%

In order to be successful, you have to make a commitment to be fully in. If you keep one foot in and the other out, you are prohibiting your success. When you make the commitment to

PEEKING BEHIND THE SCENES

jump in at 100%, you increase your success rate. I started doing this in January of 2016 and my success rate increased by 100%. Do I still fail? Yes, I do, but a lot less.

If I was able to overcome all of my life challenges to be the success that I am, if I was able to manifest my dream life, so can you.

Always remember you are worthy of living a happy, fulfilled and abundant life. There is enough abundance for everyone. Make it a point today to go after your dreams. Choose today to be that very successful person. Believe that you are worthy of being successful and that you can accomplish anything that you want.

I believe in you, and I know that you can do it! It all starts with you.

To your success!!

Symona Vitali

Symona Vitali is finally living her dream life. In 2012, she decided to move to Toronto, Canada and joined an art program where she graduated in the top 4 of her class. She is now a professional Makeup Artist, Designer and Early Childhood Educator with a certification in the Montessori field. She currently runs two successful companies. Her passion is to approach every new step in life through expressive art, resulting in happiness and inspiration. Symona is a true believer in taking action and following one's heart.

www.thenextcutestgeneration.com
www.svmakeup.com

Chapter 3

The Plan Starts by Taking Action

By Symona Vitali

Success doesn't only come from an idea. It actually comes from taking a step forward. It comes about from taking action. Sometimes this is melted and strengthened with belief, and sometimes it is just all about having faith and trusting. I truly believe that we all have a destiny, one to fulfill and to practice accomplishing, in order to reach our dreams. It is our purpose.

I was born in Toronto, Canada in the late eighties. Yet the life I grew up with, was in a small village in Bavaria, Germany, where I learned the rules of the game: go to school, graduate, and then get a job that you can be dedicated to for the rest of your life.

That was the road paved out for me then too. People had expectations of me that fit in the status quo. At the time, I accepted it, because I imagined it to be true, yet deep down inside of me I knew I wasn't made to live with standards set by others.

The path of study I had chosen was early childhood education. I moved out from my parents' home at 17. I travelled two hours to school and back every day for two years. After this, I got a job, and I relocated to a new apartment. For five years, I worked alongside other early childhood educators and observed and learned. One day, I watched one of my co-workers talking to the children like they were in the military. She followed the same program, did the same activities, sang the same songs year after year. She had been at that job for 30 years, and I could see how scared the children were of her, and how bored they were in school. I thought to myself: "That could be me in 30 years!" I had not worked this hard in school only to meet the minimum requirement as a teacher. My passion for learning was much greater. This could not be my purpose.

This was my wake up call! I was so stuck in my routine that I hadn't thought it through that far...until that moment. "That's it! I'm moving to Canada!"

Since the age of 14, I had been going to Canada to visit my Oma (my grandmother). It always pleased me to be there. It was just a different rhythm than what I was used to. Right now, I needed to be in a big city, with new people, new job opportunities, and good art schools. It seemed like the right place to be, and I would figure out my next step once I got there.

PEEKING BEHIND THE SCENES

My father, who was also born in Toronto, was always my biggest supporter. He now lives in Rome and works as an artist. I met him for the first time when I was 21. We connected instantly and shared a passion for art. He would always remind me of my goals and dreams. His words are what motivated me the most to start my life fresh, somewhere bigger than small town Germany.

I quit my job, sold my car, sold all my furniture, collected all my savings, and applied for my passport, which arrived two days before my departure. I had a one-way ticket to Toronto and no further plans ahead. At 24, I simply had a decision.

For the first few months, I lived out in Bradford (a small town outside of The Greater Toronto Area), at a family friend's place. It was very pretty, but it was very much out of the way of everything. Getting a job would be a challenge as I did not have a car to move around easily, and the closest bus stop from where I was staying was 2 km away. I had 2000 Euros with me. I never applied for any government assistance, as I wasn't even aware I was eligible for any, and I didn't even know this existed. I was living on the bare minimum so as not to run out of cash. Eventually, I was able to move in with my father's parents. I was finally in the heart of the city. I had a thousand dollars left, and I now had to make things happen in a serious way.

One day, I found myself having a great discussion with my aunt about my true passion: art and theatre! "You know, you really have a passion about this makeup thing," she said. That's when I mentioned to her that I wished there was a professional school that trained people for this. She assured me there would be such a thing in the city and recommended I searched it up.

I opened up Google and typed in two or three words relating to make up artistry and theatre, and the number one school popped up. Curious and excited, I looked into the program, and I was floored. This is what I had been looking for all my life!

I always loved art. Growing up, I would paint and draw in my room, but I always felt like this strange weirdo who had a talent I could not share with anyone. It was like no one understood what art was. In Bavaria, it was about being mechanically productive. Creativity had no space and was not accepted as a way of life in society. I felt like a fish out of water back then. Now I was getting a chance of being taught real skills I could use, plus there was an entire industry that was respectfully backing it up. I signed up for the program. It was not cheap, but it was the best 8 month program I have ever experienced! My teachers, whom were mostly males, were reputable people in the industry and had the experience and talent to go with it. They had worked on Broadway, as well as in major movies. They were bringing forward real life skills, showing me how to change people, create different characters, modifying someone's age and gender, and all sorts of other special effects all while using makeup. It was intense and so much fun. I also got to know great people from around the world who, like me, were passionate about art. I did not feel alone anymore. I felt connected to a community of like-minded people.

While in school, I still needed to find work. I was living at my grandparents rent-free, which was a blessing, but I needed pocket money. I figured since the internet helped me find my school, perhaps it could also be useful in finding connections around the city. I was looking for people to befriend here and I happen to stumble on a German meet-up group.

This took it to a whole other level for me. I was finally becoming aware of the power of networking.

I had tapped into a community of German parents who were in need of people like me: I spoke German and English, and I was great with kids. I made myself available for babysitting on weekends and made good money. I originally saw this as a short-term solution to make money while in school. What I didn't realize at the time is that I was building a powerful network as well as a powerful reputation!

What happened next was beyond my wildest dreams. I never could have come up with a better outcome by myself.

During the 8 months, I was in school, I had connected with 20 German families. Soon after I had joined the German group, I met its founder and also babysat her daughter. This lady was obviously a catalyst for good ideas. She connected me with another lady who really liked my profile and saw that I had Montessori experience. The idea of opening up a day care was born. I called her and mentioned I was in the midst of my exams for graduating from makeup artistry school. My intention was to work in the art industry upon graduation, but the daycare idea sounded interesting to me, and I would be game to help her set it up. I was then introduced to another parent who was a business owner. She did a lot of marketing and was well connected. She was the one who introduced me to the business plan. I was apprehensive in trusting her at the beginning and slept on it for two nights. After this, we set up a meeting, which my uncle and I attended together. My uncle is very business savvy, and he always has my best interest in mind. Like me, he moved from Italy to Toronto and built a new life from scratch. He helped me understand the business plan.

Mulling it through in my head for a few days made me realize how this was, in fact, an opportunity for independence.
Opening up a daycare would allow me to be my own boss, as well as move out from my grandparents' without having to be concerned about the money to cover rent every month. It was my opportunity to be independent while living in a house,

and starting my new life. A few people I knew were not as intrigued by the idea as I was and weren't particularly supportive. They did not see how it would fit into a successful plan. I made sure not to dwell on the doubts of others regarding MY future.

Looking back now, I see how mentorship has always been a big part of my road to success. My very first mentor was my maternal grandmother (Oma). She had immigrated to Canada in her early 20s. She came here with nothing. She didn't even speak the language. She built a very successful roofing business from scratch. She would teach me things, and I always found them very interesting. I loved to learn from her. She was my idol. She truly inspired me.

At the age of 25, "The next cutest Generation" Daycare had begun, and I started to learn and mold myself into a self-employed teacher. With the financial support of my family and the help from my first two clients, I purchased learning material and furniture. I was very careful in my purchases, making sure I bought Montessori products.

As time went on, I continued to build the daycare in ways I felt would benefit the children most, instead of following the exact program I saw at work in Germany. I base all the work I do on a quote from Maria Montessori: "Help me to do it myself." I strongly believe in that philosophy, and I guide my students in a way that makes them proud of their accomplishments and helps them experience their full potential. It is most important, in my opinion, for the children to have dreams starting from a young age so that they grow up with goals and follow their passion and feel confident in the skills they have. This is why I do what I do. I'm blessed that my eagerness to learn has now become a way to make a happy living.

What motivates me most is when people believe in me. I love being respected for what I do, while having the freedom of expression, to be my own boss, and not to have to fit into anyone's mold. In Germany, I used to be paid for the amount of hours I worked. Now, I feel like I get rewarded for my work. I basically get paid on value instead of time. Not only is it more profitable this way, but it is also way more satisfying and fulfilling to me.

Right now, I run the daycare during the week and on weekends and evenings I work on my make up art and design work, and often collaborate with models and photographers for various photo shoots.

Because I work from home, I make sure that when I am on vacation, and the daycare is closed, I go away with my partner. I'm so grateful for his support and couldn't have done it without him. He has always been by my side no matter how crazy my life has been. He understands how important teaching and art is for me and encourages me to never give up. Together, we feed our love for travelling and exploring other cultures and mentalities. I enjoy this and get inspired every time by it.

In 2016, we went to Bangkok over New Year's. While toasting in celebration, I reminisced about the last time I had gone away for New Year's. I reflected on how much knowledge I lacked at the time, how little I knew about business then, and how much I have grown over the last years. I have learned so much in every passing year. Each year has been like a very different and distinct chapter.

I have always made sure I make things work. I look for the path, and I don't look back, but rather learn from the experience, take the lesson, and take another step. I make sure I never get stuck on mistakes. I truly have a successful and lucrative business now. I had this bad habit of quitting when it would get hard, but I adopted a new habit and started reminding myself that I was just going to keep going, even if it was taking a lot of my energy. I am now careful on how I make decisions and I rarely go back on them. Of course I still get scared, but I make sure to not let the fear get in the way of my confidence.

Life can change in just a second! I am here to teach my next generation to live their best life on their terms.

I don't feel like what I am doing is driven by money. Obviously, it is a business, but I think it's because I'm good at what I do and I have found out how to express that to my clients. Parents know how passionate I am about teaching and how much I love it. I turned my daycare job into a creative art project. I capture the kids on camera when they learn new stuff because it's an exciting moment. I feel like I am filling in a black and white picture with colour.

I invite you to deliberately seek out your passion and find your mentors. Sometimes it's just about people reminding you of what you are capable of.
The world is yours. Go get it! You deserve it.

PEEKING BEHIND THE SCENES

Norman Douglas

Norman Douglas is an expert in car detailing. He has over 25 years of experience in the business, from being active on the floor, as well as training and mentoring. He currently owns and operates Phase II Auto Detailing in Langley, BC, Canada. Norman is a kind and honest man who has taken on the responsibility of inspiring thousands of people through morning motivational messages. He fuels himself on doing acts of kindness. His biggest strength is to bring joy and happiness to people, which he does by always going the extra mile, whether it is in business or personal.

www.phaseiiautodetailing.com

www.facebook.com/norman.douglas.5

www.facebook.com/phaseiiauto/

Chapter 4

It's all About the Attitude

By Norman Douglas

Anything is possible when you have the right mindset and the right attitude. I have experienced this many times myself. I have lived through the most unlikely scenarios, yet I never let anything or anyone stop me, especially not my own circumstances. There is always an open road somewhere. It is simply yours to find, and once you do, then it is for you to decide to travel on it.

I am a true entrepreneur! It's in my blood and in my heart. I was born in a family of business makers and business runners: my parents had a grocery store and a rum bar in Jamaica. This ownership of self, as well as good work ethics, were ingrained in me early.

The first business I started was an electrical company in Jamaica: Transformer World Ltd. rewiring and manufacturing transformers. My first paycheque was $45. I remember how disappointed my partner felt. I had to remind him to be grateful that we still earned something and that now we had to work hard to grow it. We turned it into a very successful company that was eventually earning thirty thousand dollars a week.

It was so successful that we were privy to two robberies. I was involved in both of them. The first time, I was alone in the shop. The second time, everyone was there. It happened in broad daylight. There was a shootout. One guy got hit by a bullet and was dead on the spot. That's when my mom, who had been living in Canada since 1974, said to me: "Norman, it's time for you to leave Jamaica."

In the fall of 1988, Hurricane Gilbert hit the island, and in December of that year, I had made my mother's wish come true.

Arriving in Canada in the winter was a big turn off. I didn't like it here. I told my mom I was going back home, because I liked working outside and this weather wasn't conducive to it. I felt like I was taken to prison. I felt restricted in what I could do. I was so determined to go back that I didn't unpack my suitcase for a year.

Upon my arrival in Toronto, I got myself a job working at the post office at night, sorting mail. I was not making enough money, and the work was boring for me. One day I told my manager I was quitting in order to join my brother's start-up: a car cleaning business.

PEEKING BEHIND THE SCENES

The manager was mad!

I am a good worker. I am the type to be shown what to do once or twice and then I like to do it on my own. If you give me 5 hours to do something, I will make sure I do it well in less than the allocated time. I'm autonomous that way and I like a challenge.

My post office manager asked me if I could stay on for 6 more months to train someone to do my job, so I did. After the 6 months, not wanting to lose me as an employee, he asked if I was really sure I wanted to pursue this business "thing" with my brother and offered me more money to stay.
My mind was made up! I needed to be my own boss.

I started working with my brother, but shortly thereafter, he left to go to school and pursue a career in aviation. I was left alone to take this car cleaning business to the next level. I could see there was money to be made here. It was a lot of work when I started. I was charging too little. Many days I told myself I wasn't really sure what I was doing, but I kept reminding myself that I was going to make it. My wife was always there to encourage me, even when I could not see how this was possible. She stood by me the entire time. I worked hard and kept the learning up along the way.

I started to make projections and was going to raise my price by 15% every year. After one year, I did just that: I raised my price. I lost some business, but again, I was determined, and I learned new ways. I put my pride aside and did what was necessary to get business. I went to the dealerships and approached them with my sale's pitch to give me a car to do, and if they didn't like the end result, I wouldn't call them, and they wouldn't call me. Some turned me away, but of those who gave me a try, all were satisfied and loved what I had done. I was moving forward.

One day, a lady came to my shop. She wanted to interview me and asked if I minded being published in the paper. Next thing I knew, the phone was ringing off the hook. I had been featured in the Toronto Star, and people were coming in from the other end of the city to have their car detailed at my shop. Everyone started treating me like a celebrity.

The company grew steadily. I went from charging 40$ a car to now averaging 280$ a car. Not only was I making good money and growing my business, but I was also growing a great reputation and a wonderful network. In fact, to this day, all the high-end detailers in Toronto have been trained by me. I had truly become the expert in this business. I kept up with what was happening in the market, which products were available, how I could use them to enhance what I was already doing, in order to deliver an even better service.

PEEKING BEHIND THE SCENES

One thing I learned growing up as a young businessman is that you have to befriend the right people: the ones who think like you and who want to grow. That will help you, because when you converse with them, they will always have ideas to share. You can learn from those ideas and apply them to your business in whatever way you need.

Everything was good.

And then...life happened.

I got into a car accident. My shoulder was badly injured and needed some major repair through surgical procedures. I went through with it as well as with the long recovery process that followed. Shortly after, the location I had for my business in Toronto was not renewing my lease. The place was being rezoned for residential purposes. This, in conjunction with my surgery and recuperation to health, left me with little time and energy to pursue continuing on with this successful business. It eventually closed.

In 2009, we moved to Florida and were ready to start over again. Unfortunately, our timing was not ideal. Florida was in a recession then. We eventually packed up to return to Canada. This time, our destination was Vancouver. It was a place we had never been before, a place we knew no one in, and also the warmest city in Canada! People questioned how I could pack up the entire family and just move somewhere brand new, with no roots, no plan, no job, nothing.

My logic was that God made birds that are capable of migrating. They move, they adapt, they survive. I also know that God gave me more wisdom than a bird. I too can move, adapt, and do more than survive.

It was evident to me that once I got to Vancouver, I would be starting the same business from scratch. I knew detailing. Not only did I have the expertise, but now I also had many years of business experience and knowledge behind me. I had a clear advantage. I started with basic research: I walked into various detailing places to get my car cleaned. I soon realized they didn't have a clue what they were doing. "Woah!" I knew there was a market here! Again, a confirmation of my clear advantage.

I found a location that happened to be near all the high-end car dealerships. We blended in quite nicely. People actually thought we were one of the dealerships.
How does this happen? By having high standards. We represent a brand that is professional and clean. We have a nice reception area, everyone wears a uniform, so we are clean and on the same page, and we build on team effort. When we work as a team: we rise together, and we fall together. There are no weak links present. I hire quality people, and I lead by

example. I'm on the floor with them every day, working just as hard as they do. I need to be the one responsible for setting the tone. This way, my employees have something to base their standards of performance on. We also worship God every morning before the start of our day. It helps to lift the spirits of everyone, to solidify us as a team, and to start a fresh page together every morning.

Every two weeks, we hold a meeting to make sure everyone is informed on what is happening and to assure quality by keeping the staff up to date with any training and new methods that can be implemented. We can paint, remove scratches, and even bring the car back to its original smell. We go above and beyond car detailing.

I passionately love what I do, and I want my employees to feel pride in what they do too. I also love to see the joy on my customer's faces when they come and pick up their vehicle. It's not even about the money, because if somebody is not satisfied, I don't feel happy taking their money. I feel great joy within when they are astonished by the difference they see, and they can truly say "wow!"

I was never big on advertising. In Toronto, I had only used the yellow pages. And now, in Vancouver, I was still using the yellow pages as well as strategically positioning myself on google.

This time, I didn't have to go looking for business. Business came to us. Which makes it better, easier.

Our first big customer came in while we were still setting up. A guy from a neighbouring dealership walked in the day we were putting up our sign and asked if we were ready for business, because he was ready to start sending us cars.

When we were first opening in Vancouver, my wife said to me: "Norman how are we going to get the jobs?" I told her about this quarterly I had been reading. This Christian man had a business that he promoted only with God and that He would send the Angels to find him work. I also told her that my plan was to do the same as this man had done. She didn't say anything, but I could tell from her facial expression that the only words that echoed in her head at the time were: "Are you crazy?!?"

Yet, she didn't question. She trusted.

The next morning at the shop, we had ten dealerships knocking at our door saying they had "heard about us".

I have always been a man of Faith, but since, I actually work on the principle of God. I trust in God, and I worry about nothing.

I believe that God sent us that location. We have been opened for business for a year and a half, and we haven't experienced a slow day since.

PEEKING BEHIND THE SCENES

In fact, we don't open Saturdays, because it's the day of the Sabbath. Saturday we worship Him. Saturday is also the day that most people get their errands done for the week. People are busy on Saturdays. But Sundays, that's when most people take the day to relax or clean their house and cook for the week and do other housebound chores. It's easier for them to drop off their car with us in the morning and have it returned to them clean by day's end. I'm the only detailing shop that is open on Sundays, and I am jammin' on those days. When you honour God, he honours you!

I really love what I do. I love to help people, and I like to see people happy. I even help people get jobs in Canada in just about any industry. Business is about people! Staying in constant communication and growth are important concepts. There is always something new with technology; it's important to stay ahead. You have to do research on a regular basis to keep ahead of the game. If you are not growing, you are dying. Growing keeps you active: it keeps your body and your mind active. It keeps you youthful and fulfilled. It also keeps you producing.

My next step very much involves growth: my dream is to open up a successful franchise in every province within the next five years. I know it will happen.
I encourage you to also pursue your dreams. Don't let your current circumstances hold you back. With steady dedication, you too can flourish from your passion. God Bless.

Ms. Pino

Ms. Pino has received numerous compliments for her creative ways to become successful, as well as for her insights in implementing innovative ideas and making money, especially in Real Estate. Now, she is enjoying her Online Business as well.

She is an Investor, Real Estate Developer, Self-Published Author and Online TV-Host of her own live stream show.
Ms. Pino is a Certified Trainer, Coach, Mentor and Mastermind Facilitator.

She personally teaches her proven "Millionaire Approach System" to Business Owners and Entrepreneurs who want to Master the Game of Marketing, Advertising & Sales.
Ms. Pino is currently enjoying her passion: "Helping others become Successful".

Visit her website: www.mspino.com
Facebook: www.facebook.com/mspinolive
Twitter: www.twitter.com/mspinolive

PEEKING BEHIND THE SCENES

Chapter 5

Self-Empowerment:
That's the Secret Sauce in the Journey to Success

By Ms. Pino

The journey to success is a road often traveled by many, yet mostly achieved by just a few. Why? ...because usually people give up too soon. They get tired. They get frustrated. They want instant gratification. They find it too difficult. They find it too challenging. They find it too expensive. They get emotionally drained. They get uninspired.

I am here to tell you that when you know what you want, when you are sure of your inner desires and when you know deep inside that you can achieve whatever you want... success is guaranteed!

I know this because I have been there. I have already done that. I build on my success on a daily basis, regardless of how successful I might think I am... especially when I am passionate about what I do.

And I am here with the intention to teach you, to inspire you and to ignite your heart, wherever you are in your life right now, wherever you are in your business right now, and wherever you are in the world right this minute.

I have been an entrepreneur and a business owner for over 22 years. As a Cuban immigrant, I started from zero. I arrived from Cuba with the dress I was wearing and an old brown bag with my childhood photos. My family didn't have any money. They made up for it by giving us tons of love and instilling great family values. I learned to discover the magic in self-empowerment. I am ready to share with you 3 stories that I have never shared before until now.

Story #1: What does it take to get to your first million?

The idea of becoming a millionaire had been on my mind ever since I was 12 or 13 years old. I used to dream about big houses, nice cars, and going on luxury vacations when I was back in Cuba. Of course, the pictures that appeared in my mind were the images I remembered from the old American movies I used to watch on Saturday night on an old black and white television that had noisy and squeaky audio.

I believed that one day I would be walking down Central Park in New York, while waiting for a Comedy show to start. I believed that one day I would be vacationing in Miami Beach in one of the most expensive hotels. I believed that one day I would be living in a beautiful house, where I would feel as if I would be in a five star hotel. I really believed that one day I would be a millionaire.

As a very young woman, how could I make this dream come true?

At 15 years old, I got pregnant with my son Victor. My dreams got stronger, because I wanted to give my son the very best. I was studying Civil Construction during the day, and English in the evenings. Life was good in my eyes. I was building the foundation to my bright future. At 20, I arrived in the USA to make my dreams happen. It wasn't easy, but for sure it was all worth it.

I only had 3 jobs in my entire life before I started to work independently. I built my first company, made some money and I failed. I built my second company, made even more money and I failed even harder. I continued in the quest. I built my third company, made substantial income to live comfortably, but it didn't take long before I realized that what I was doing wasn't making me happy. I was working 12-15 hour days, 7 days a week. And still I was so far from reaching that million-dollar mark.

Was that the so-called American dream? Because for me it felt more like the American-Hell-dream.

It was time to re-think my strategy. What else could I do that could make me that first million? What could I leverage in such a way that I could reach my dream... and truly live it!
Then, I remembered that I knew construction. I started to look for opportunities in the real estate industry. I did some research. I talked to some general contractors. I decided that I would become a Real Estate Developer! Voilà!

But, I had no money to invest in such magnitude, no contacts, no previous experience. However, I did have a burning desire to go through the challenge. I invested every cent I had and borrowed all I could. I worked day and night, 7 days a week for over 18 months. I struggled to even cover my rent, to pay my electric bill and to put food on the table. I thought that if I was able to build at least 4 homes, I would be able to sell them and make my first million.

There were times when it was so bad, that we had to get a bucket of water from the lake to flush the toilets, because we had our electricity cut off as well as our city water. My landlord at the time, God bless her heart, was very patient until one day, she put the 3-day eviction notice on my door. The kids (Victor was around 15 and Joshua, my wife's son was around 7) were such good sports about the whole situation.

PEEKING BEHIND THE SCENES

They enjoyed grilled chicken wings, grilled hamburgers, grilled corn, grilled everything. That was what we had at the time.

Patience. Persistence. Passion. Faith. Belief. Unconditional Love.

Work. Work. Work. Work. And more work. Things turned around: It felt like magic!

One contract. Then another one. Then many more followed. One private investor agreed to give me my first loan. Many more followed. One lot was bought. Then 256 lots of 1 1/2 acre each were bought. One home was built. Then another. And the first 6 homes allowed me to reach my first million.

That was just the beginning. Over the course of the next 5 years, our company had sold over $68,000,000 in new construction.

Life was good. Life was perfect. Life had showed me that when I work hard and I believe in myself, anything is possible.

Story #2: How to Self-Empower yourself when chaos is all you've got?

It is May 11, 2006. I am sleeping. Far away, I hear a banging at the door of my master bedroom. I hear voices. I am half asleep. I am half awake. After a few short moments, I realize I am awake. I hear my name. I hear my father's voice calling my name. I instinctively jump from the bed. I run to open the door. I see my father. I also see my mother. They are both crying. They both rush over to me. They hug me. I am totally confused. I ask: "What happened?" I see tears in their eyes and a deep sadness that I couldn't understand. My father says: "It's Victor. He had an accident." then I ask: "Is he ok? Is he fine?" My father answers: "No, he is gone!"

I simply could not even process what I had just heard. My son. My life. My reason to thrive, to fight, to exceed, to succeed... gone? That was by far the most unbearable day of my entire life. My 19 year old Victor had a motorcycle accident and there we were not knowing how to deal with such pain. It certainly was excruciating.

Even writing these lines now, it is not easy to share this story. I don't like to publicly share this. Only my closest friends and family and a selected few know of my hidden truth that I carried bottled up inside of me for so long. Now, 10 years after his passing and endless hours of dealing with my broken heart, I am here to tell you that self-empowerment was the only solution I found in order to put my heart back together.

When I hear people complaining about the economy, their jobs, their finances, their relationships, I think to myself how superficial they are. It amazes me how people waste their time and their lives in bullshit. I think that if they only took the time to invest in understanding themselves better, most if not all of their problems, would go away.

As a result of the instant and drastic change my life took, I had to really really really look inside myself and make sense of my chaos. How was I going to give my life meaning? What about purpose? Honestly, I didn't know.
This 10 year journey of my own self-discovery has taught me to pay attention to what is truly important in my life and in the lives of others around me.

I have noticed how people walk around in pain, suffering and grieving. Some, like me, have lost a loved one. Others grieve over losing their job, their relationships, their status-quo, their money, their fame. Go figure!

I am here to tell you to start asking yourself: "What is it that I want in my life today, right now?"
When you answer this question to the highest level of integrity within yourself, you will discover that life will shift

for you. You will see the world full of possibilities, full of opportunities, full of life, abundance and happiness wherever you go in the world.

You will only focus your time and energy on those activities that will help you feel really good. You will understand the power of LOVING UNCONDITIONALLY. For me, that was the biggest lesson. Learning to love myself unconditionally, learning to love the world again, learning to laugh again, learning to live my life with meaning and true purpose. Believe me when I tell you that it is possible!

So, go out there in your world and follow your dream. Follow your passion. Make the commitment right now to do whatever it takes to be happy and prosperous. Life is fragile. Do not take it for granted. Life is a gift. Make yours worth living. Like I always say in my live stream TV show: "Laugh. Learn. Live at your Best every single day of your existence. You deserve it. I deserve it. We all deserve it!!!"

Story #3: How to build your Legacy?

When life puts you to the test, you have a choice: you either contract or you decide to push forward and expand. I have opted for total and complete expansion. Like many other successful entrepreneurs, I have learned that there are always new ideas, new opportunities. How do you want to be remembered? What do you want people to say about you when you are gone? What legacy do you want to leave behind?

Please think about it now, because the answer you come up with will dictate the quality of life you will have in the next day, in the next week, in the next month, in the next year...and before you know it, you will have a lifetime of memories, a lifetime of experiences, a lifetime of learnings. The question will be: "Did I live? Did I love? Did I matter?", just like Brendon Burchard says.

I had thought about this legacy topic when I first started building the homes. I thought about it even more seriously when I started to develop my current business: my online TV network.

After the real estate industry slowed down back in 2010, I decided it was time to let go, to sell, to take some time off and to reorganize my life. It was also around the same time that I had started to question and think about what would interest me again, what would turn me on again, what would inspire me again.

One afternoon, while I was sitting in my home-office at my first ever built new home, I found myself contemplating a gorgeous sunset. Through the wide and open window, I could see the different tonalities of reds, yellows, and oranges. The clear blue sky was getting ready to receive the warm summer evening. The trees were magnificent. The countryside view was simply spectacular. I had a spark in my heart. I felt a sudden emotion to do something new. I had the idea of starting a new business.

I went back to my original question: "What is it that I want in my life today, right now?" and immediately answered: "I want a business that I love doing every day, that I can build from anywhere in the world, and that can make me millions of dollars. I want a business where I can help a lot of people become happier and more prosperous."

That was it! The next day, I started building the new dream. Currently, this chapter is an essential stepping stone for making my dream come true. Will I make it? You bet I will, because when I know what I truly want, success is guaranteed!

I understand it will take me some time. So far, I have learned so much about the online world. I was completely technology challenged when I started this business. I didn't know anything about blogging, how to upload a video, which platforms to use. I didn't even know how to explain my business. I didn't know my message nor who my ideal client was, or even how to monetize my idea. I didn't even feel that this was a real business.

PEEKING BEHIND THE SCENES

Despite the challenges I faced, I took the road less traveled. I decided to learn, to give myself the chance to discover the magic, and to see for myself if what I had envisioned in my mind was even possible.

What I found has dazzled me! I have found that when I create a business where I lovingly and compassionately include others and myself collectively, I think big, I think huge, I think globally, I think legacy!

What makes me extremely happy is that every day I have the opportunity to share my vision, my voice, my heart, my happiness, my message with millions of people around the world.

By the time you will be reading these lines, I am sure I will have already surpassed a million views in my Online TV platform. Most likely over 500 live stream shows, which means over 500 different topics, different messages to teach you, to inspire you and to ignite your heart wherever you are in your life right now, wherever you are in your business right now and wherever you are in the world. I cordially invite you to tune in to my daily LIVE show by visiting www.mspinolive.com

Also, I want to invite you to start building your own legacy. You have a message to share with the world. You have expertise that others need. You have answers to other people's problems. You can inspire others to follow their dreams. I know that together we can change and will change millions of people's lives.

Start today!

PEEKING BEHIND THE SCENES

Dr. Lauren E. Karatanevski, DC

Over the past two decades, Dr. Lauren Karatanevski has functioned in a variety of roles that include an evidence-based chiropractic practitioner, certified kinesiologist, personal trainer, elite athlete, entrepreneur and network marketing professional.

She is the clinic owner of the Back in Action Health Clinic as well as the Oakville Optihealth Clinic.

Dr. Lauren is passionate and committed to creating an environment that allows her patients to deal with pain, increase their mobility, optimize their health, prevent injury, increase participation in activities of daily living as well as work toward achieving a pain free fully functioning lifestyle.

www.drlaurenk.com
Facebook: https://www.facebook.com/drlaurenbia?ref=hl
Instagram: @drlaurenbia

Chapter 6

Blood, Sweat and Success

By: Dr. Lauren E. Karatanevski, DC

I was born a Canadian of European decent. Over fifty years ago, both sets of my grandparents and my father immigrated to Canada in search of a better life. They left Macedonia (part of the former Yugoslavia) as humble farmers, and moved to a country where they were told; they would be provided with better opportunities for their family. They started from nothing, with only the clothes on their back. They were undistinguished foreigners, barely spoke English, and were illiterate. Starting off they worked in factories and shined shoes for a living, making approximately $0.25 an hour. When my parents got married, my mother worked two jobs – one as an elementary school teacher, and the other as a cashier at Loblaws. My father worked as a service manager with Famous Players Theatres. My non-English speaking great-grandmother lived with my parents, sister, and me. We all lived in a modest house. My great-grandmother and I shared a room and a queen-size bed. We weren't rich nor did we come from money. I was rooted with a traditional and humble upbringing; and because of that, I was taught to work hard, save my money and spend wisely.

Where I am now...

I am 32 years old. I am an Investor, Chiropractor, Business Owner, Network Marketing Professional, International Best Selling Author, and Entrepreneur. At the age of 21, I started building my investment portfolio. My mother had purchased *Rich Dad, Poor Dad* by Robert Kiyosaki as a Christmas gift for me to read. I think she bought it for the title, however what she didn't know was that this book would be the catalyst to my love for educating myself about building my financial independence. The book chronicles Kiyosaki's childhood upbringing and the different attitudes between his biological father "poor dad" and his friend's father "rich dad" on the importance of increasing your financial savviness in wealth building, investing, and business ownership. At one point in the book, Kiyosaki outlines how one could start investing a minimal amount of money at the age of 18 and with continued smart investing, could be a millionaire at the time of retirement. I was 3 years late!!! It was at that moment I started investing in Tax Free Savings, Guaranteed Investment Certificates, Mutual Funds, Registered Retirement Savings Plans and the Stock Market. Rather than spending the money I got for birthdays, for Christmas and special occasions, I invested what little I had to diversify my portfolio and started saving for my future.

PEEKING BEHIND THE SCENES

I attended the University of North Carolina and received a degree in Kinesiology and Chemistry. I also represented the University in their Swimming and Diving Program. In February 2008, I represented Macedonia at the World Championships/Olympic Trials on the three meter springboard. I graduated with a Doctor of Chiropractic Medicine from the Canadian Memorial Chiropractic College in June 2012.

In September of 2012, I purchased my first multidisciplinary healthcare facility with Scott (my fiancé) called Back in Action Health Clinic in Toronto, Canada.

In January 2014, we started another multidisciplinary healthcare facility called the Oakville Optihealth Clinic in Oakville, Canada.

In October of 2014, I started a network marketing business as a plan to help people support their health and wellness goals as well as to help educate and mentor people in believing they are capable of owning their own business.

In February 2016, I was given the opportunity to co-author in a book called *Manifesting a New Life - Your Magical Guide to Attracting the Life You Want,* which reached the International Best Seller list in its first day of sales.

Compiled by **JENNIFER LOW**

Why am I telling you this?...

My purpose is not to glorify my accomplishments, accolades or business ventures, but rather to show you that anything is possible no matter where you come from in life.

If you had just read my accomplishments without me detailing my history, you may have believed I grew up with a silver spoon in my mouth. You may have thought to yourself, I could never achieve success, because my path growing up in life was much different. You may have even thought that success is gifted to those who come from a gifted upbringing. My history shows quite the opposite. I am a prodigy of immigrant grandparents, and extremely hard working parents. I was given many opportunities to find my own path in life, to experience my own hardships (and learn from them), and to achieve my own success.

Blood, Sweat and the truth about success...

My hope for you is to enlighten you that success is not what you see on the surface, but rather comes from a foundation of hard work, strength, persistence, determination, dedication and stubbornness. I hope to show you that success is not due to inadequate genetics or resources. The information you will receive has been taken from many scientific resources, which will outline that success and achieving expert performance comes from deliberate practice, and the importance of constructive feedback. Lastly, it will also show that we have the ability and potential to be successful and create success for ourselves.

Blood

"Be not afraid of greatness. Some are born great, some achieve greatness, and some have greatness thrust upon 'em."
- William Shakespeare, Twelfth Night

What I love most about Shakespeare's romantic comedy, *Twelfth Night*, is that although it was published over 400 years ago, the themes of the play still resonate today with the hardships that we face in our own quest for success and greatness: wanting a different path in life, to be successful, and to be someone other than who we are. The quote above depicts the point in the play where Marvolio, a delusional and hopeless steward, finds a note which he believes to be from the woman he loves, Countess Olivia. Marvolio wishes and dreams to be of noble blood and is told in the letter to act, speak, and dress as if he were a man of nobility. The end of the letter (and what I found to be more profound than the quote above) tells Marvolio that his happy new life is within his reach. If he doesn't want it, he can continue acting like a helpless servant who is not brave enough to achieve the happiness before him. Dreaming and wishing to be great and successful is not a new concept. We all dream for a life where we matter, where we can make a difference to ourselves and to others, and where we are successful. Maybe we need to be asking ourselves, if greatness and success can be achieved, to what lengths do we have to go to achieve it?

The Story of Ted Williams...

I read the story of one of baseball's all-time great players, Ted Williams, in a book called *The Genius in All of Us*, by David Shenk. In his book, Shenk discusses how conventional theorists believe people are separated in two categories: the genetically gifted and the genetically limited. To these theorists, the genetically gifted are those born with genetic gifts and talents. People like LeBron James, Henry Matisse, and Ludwig van Beethoven are incredibly talented individuals who at a young age, excelled at their given activity/domain. The genetically limited are those with no genetic gifts or talents - they are ordinary people who are limited in their ability to accomplish or excel at any given activity/domain. By utilizing scientific research from many different fields, Shenk explains that extraordinarily talented people are not only genetically gifted, but that it is a combination of genes and environment that make a person talented and successful. He also states that through this intermingling (genes and environment) we can take ownership of our accomplishments and successes.

PEEKING BEHIND THE SCENES

Ted Williams was considered a baseball legend and a God on the field. People and broadcasters believed he was born with the genetic ability to be an outstanding baseball hitter: phenomenal eye-hand coordination, laser-like eyesight, muscular grace, and unparalleled baseball instincts. If you were to ask Ted Williams about his superhuman abilities in baseball he would explain that it was not genetic. "Nothing except practice, practice, practice will bring out that ability." He went on to say, "The reason I saw things was that I was so intense. It was [super] discipline, not super eyesight," and "I wasn't going to let anything stop me from being the hitter I hoped to be." As a child and into his adolescence, Williams grew up in the absence of his parents. With no parental guidance and influence, Williams looked toward baseball as an outlet away from his dysfunctional home. At the age of six, he found refuge at the baseball diamond, two blocks away from his family house. He would hit baseballs every waking hour of every day, year after year. His friends would remark, "His whole life was hitting the ball. He always had that bat in his hand." When Ted Williams was drafted into professional baseball, his hard work and determination did not stop there. He would be the first to show up for practice and the last to leave. Following a practice, Williams would ask his coach for all the used game balls. When asked why he would need those balls, he remarked - for a little extra hitting after he finished with supper. Williams believed and insisted his achievements were the sum of what he had put into the game. Ted Williams was neither genetically gifted nor superhuman. Ted Williams worked single-mindedly for his baseball success. He LIVED and BREATHED baseball... that is how he became one of baseball's greatest. If we all have it within us to be successful - why is it that some of us are more successful than others?

Sweat

"It's supposed to be hard. If it were easy, everyone would do it."
- Tom Hanks in A League of Their Own
Practice does not make Perfect or Successful... The Concept of Deliberate Practice

According to the research conducted by Anders Ericsson, Professor of Psychology from Florida State University, the ability of an individual to achieve extraordinary success can be attained through *deliberate practice*. In his research article entitled, *The Role of Deliberate Practice in the Acquisition of Expert Performance*, Ericsson explains that Deliberate Practice is the concept of highly structured activity, where the goal is to improve performance. He notes that "maximization of deliberate practice is neither short-lived nor simple. It extends over a period of time of at least 10 years and involves optimization within several constraints."

PEEKING BEHIND THE SCENES

Deliberate Practice - Simply Put

Deliberate Practice is a form of highly structured activity with the goal of improving performance. It is practice of a given task or skill that requires energy, time and a full-time commitment. A coach, mentor or teacher is used to offer constructive criticism and give explicit instruction on how to improve on that task or skill so the individual is able to diagnose their errors and improve upon them. The end goal of deliberate practice is achieved when the individual becomes a professional and has made a significant contribution in their given field.

Who practices deliberately?

It is often that we see elite level athletes undergo deliberate practice. At a young age these children are plucked out of a crowd of aspiring athletes, because they exhibit some sort of "talent". Their parents enrol them in a program where they are coached and monitored by professionals. Quite often these athletes will train 6 hours a day, 5-7 days a week. They have made a commitment to perform on a full-time basis with the end goal being that of high-level performance.

The Constraints - Why People May Not Ever Achieve Expert Performance or Success...What People Don't See...

1. Deliberate Practice requires a considerable amount of time, money and energy. It also requires access to teachers, training material and training facilities.
2. Deliberate Practice is not motivating.
3. Deliberate practice is an effortful activity.
4. The mere repetition of an activity will not automatically lead to improvement
5. In the absence of the feedback loop, efficient learning is impossible and improvement is minimal.

A Personal Note...An Example of Deliberate Practice in the Workforce

When I first started my practice four years ago, I made a full-time commitment to myself and to my patients that I would always be there for them and their care. I worked deliberately 12 hours a day, 5 days a week. When I had no patients in the clinic, I remained at the clinic for the entire 12 hour day and worked on business strategies in order to generate more patients for the practice. When I got home after my 12 hour day, I continued working on improving my skills and business strategies until I went to bed. I educated myself by taking courses on patient care, business management, and treatment strategies. I sought out the advice from mentors on how to improve as a chiropractor. I have been peer-reviewed on my practice skills and note taking, and I have learned from those who have been in the business much longer than me. I have repeated all of those tasks over and over again for the last four years.

My results: I own two multidisciplinary chiropractic clinics. We have a constant referral source in our clinic from medical doctors, patients and reviews from the internet. Lastly, I have been asked to mentor and teach students about building a chiropractic practice. SUCCESS!

Success

"Successful and unsuccessful people do not vary greatly in their abilities. They vary in their desires to reach their potential."
- John Maxwell

The take-home message I would like to leave you with -- There is no difference between you and the next person in being successful. It is evident in the examples in this chapter that we are all capable of success. How you will differ from your family, friends, or colleagues starts with believing in yourself and your abilities, and continues with you working toward those beliefs. Achieving success is not an immediate outcome, but rather a long term process. It requires constant hard work, deliberate practice, constructive criticism, constant sacrifice, relentless dedication and focused determination.

Being successful is a mindset. You have to want it bad enough, and do whatever it takes to achieve it. Success is not material. Success comes from accomplishing your goals.

Remember... There is no such thing as a glass ceiling in your ability to be successful. YOU are the ONLY person who will determine your own success.

My Wish for You!...

My wish for all of you is that you see that you are capable of anything you set your mind to, capable of anything you dare to dream and capable of living the life you want.

- Dr. Lauren Karatanevski, DC

References:
Shenk, David., *The Genius in all of Us.* First Anchor Books Edition, March 2011.
Ericsson, Anders., *The Role of Deliberate Practice in the Acquisition of Expert Performance.*, Psychological Review 1993, Vol. 100. No. 3, 363-406

PEEKING BEHIND THE SCENES

Jennifer Low

Jennifer has always loved to write and is now pursuing this more actively as a writer, compiler, editor, and ghostwriter. She is an international best-selling author and has been published several times.

Jennifer is committed to respectful empowerment and is dedicated to adding polish to people who are seeking that higher standard. She does this in the writing world, as well as through coaching and mentoring. Jennifer is helping people realize their true potential, reach their goals and achieve true success. She is also an excellent mother and a great investor.

You can contact her at:
www.anauthenticu.com
www.facebook.com/anauthenticu/
www.linkedin.com/in/jennifer-low-812a2716

Chapter 7

Success was always there:
I just had to open my eyes!

By Jennifer Low

We all have a different definition of success. I believe mine, like most, was tied to money. We have a tendency to associate success to a visually opulent lifestyle: the nice house, the nice cars, the frequent vacations, and perhaps even a high-end education. It is important to remember that money attribution is always a choice of priorities often based on one's personal values and beliefs. Getting back to success itself, what I have found is that unless people have reached fame and fortune status they often do not consider themselves successful. I am guilty of this too. Many of us seem to wait for that one moment when we have crossed the finish line to "the big life" and can breathe a sigh of relief. It often times comes across that way for the person looking in; yet for the one who is seeking, reaching, and striving for that success, the picture looks much different.

As I grew and expanded my life and focused more on success, I realized that my perception on that topic had completely mutated. I believe the road to success starts with deliberate choice, simply making a decision, then committing to making it happen, while keeping a relentless appetite for it. Success is made up of every little step you take. It's about doing the daily tasks that will bring you to your desired results. It never happens over night, but rather through rhythm and grace, habit, rituals …and time!

Having said all this, my personal story of success is ironically very much related to money.

Let me start at the beginning… I had my first child in 1993 and have been a stay at home mom since. Nothing was more important to me then to raise my own offspring in an environment of love, while setting them up for success in any way I could. In my mind, the success of my children had to do with developing their brain for constant expansion, gearing them towards independence in their decision making processes, as well as making sure they were equipped with great self-esteem and confidence, enough for them to be assured they would never be afraid to do something new and always be guided to explore and stretch themselves for more.

I absolutely adored being a stay at home mom. I cautiously poured every best piece of me into these human beings I had created. I felt it was my responsibility to set them up to live fully, right from the beginning. To me it was my job and I took it very seriously. My only downfall was that I was not getting paid to do it, and hence not making any money. I chose not to focus on that as I was cared for very well by my husband who worked long long hours to build his business, and I felt fulfilled by the mom-work I was doing.

The problematic of my financial dependency came to haunt me in 2008. While in Spain with the kids for two weeks, I received an email that said he had been to see a lawyer. Anxiety invaded me so badly I couldn't sleep that night. I felt sickened to the core. I had return tickets home in 3 days, only I didn't know what "home" I was coming back to. I imagined he had changed the locks and I'd be stranded with the kids on the front porch upon our arrival with no back up plan available. I had no family in town and no personal bank account to speak of. Oh, so much went through my mind that night and the following 3 days. Fortunately, they were just thoughts.

None of that actually happened. Instead, we continued to cohabitate as a couple for a few months and then he moved out that December. I remained in the house for an additional two and a half years. The idea was to create a smooth transition for the children from the parental split and the family dissolving. As parents, we figured that gradual change would not be as devastating and it would help minimize the emotional impact it may have on them.

During those two and a half years post split, the idea of making money, and being able to provide, somehow became an obsession to me. I was now on my own. I had to depend on me! As much as I loved that house, it had a ten thousand dollar mortgage payment a month on it and it was expensive to run on the daily. On no income this caused me much stress. I was open to ideas and always on the look out for solutions.

Having grown up in the love and ease of having multiple languages at my disposal I signed up for my third University degree as an initial knee jerk reaction: this time in Translation.
I could easily do that type of work from home. I was not afraid to work. The priority was for my schedule to remain flexible in order to still be available for the children. At the same time, I joined a network marketing company. The business model made too much sense to me, and the company had many very successful people I would meet up with on a weekly basis.
I saw possibilities.

The execution of either of these two choices I had taken on, however, wasn't going to be as easy as I had first imagined. My kids were at school during the day, yet my classes all took place in the evening. As for the home-based business, I figured I knew so many people there was no way I could fail. Oh, did I have much to learn! I knew nothing about sales and I had this naive thinking that my so-called friends would support me. I was in for a rude awakening.

PEEKING BEHIND THE SCENES

Obstacles – obstacles – obstacles

What this entire process did produce is someone who's desire to grow, succeed and achieve, exponentially exploded. The more resistance I encountered, the harder I gave of myself. Falling victim to my circumstances was a choice. I chose not to live in defeat. Ever!

Instead, I took personal responsibility and I started analyzing what I lacked in skills and knowledge and picked up books, audios, videos, and attended seminars that would fill up my knowledge cup and my insatiable thirst for growth. I wanted to become that person who could do absolutely anything I put my mind to and then apply it into a successful endeavor. I wanted to feel victorious within myself. The desire for self-satisfaction and fulfillment is what constantly drove me, and it is still fueling me today.

I felt I had so much to catch up on when I was first on my own, I did not know where to start. One of the places I felt like I lacked in most, was in financial education. So I started there. And since I wanted to be making money and managing money I felt I needed to know what money truly was.

I found a financial mentor in Robert Kiyosaki. I devoured any and all information he offered in his books. I didn't always understand it. Some concepts were a little too advanced for me at the time as I was really starting from a blank slate state. Growing up, my money role models were most obviously my parents. My mom had been a big big saver all her life. To compensate for it, my dad took the other side of that coin and was a gambler. I understood each of those standpoints and agreed with neither of them. Instead, I took what I could from Robert and mulled it over, repeated it in my head until it actually made sense, and looked for real life examples of application all around me in my every day living.

Suddenly, I was looking at the world through a new pair of lenses. The colours were different, the depths were different, the point of reference (ie. the mindset) was different.
It was the same life only now I was seeing it through a different looking glass.

As time progressed, our 20 years together as a couple was being wrapped up in a beautiful and pricy bow. The assets were being divvied up.

I had learned a lot from this entire legal process. Thanks to many of the Robert Kiyosaki teachings I understood the why behind much of the inner workings of the financial life I had lived over the course of our years of marriage. I finally found logic in why my ex had done certain things with the monies. Again, I didn't agree with all of them, but I had seen much of it in application and in action. I was grateful for it even though I was having trouble wrapping my head around my current situation. My perspective was still so, that I was privileged to have been exposed to it in the first place. Now it was merely about processing it fully and moving forward with more education.

A few years later, when I came in contact with larger sums of money I knew exactly what to do with it. I understood the concept of allowing the goose to lay the golden eggs and to live on the eggs alone. As long as the goose was alive it would keep laying eggs. Now it was a matter of finding the right team of investors to help me manage my money the way I wanted it to and in the style that suited me best. Seven years after the initial unfolding, I was making enough passive income to pay for the basic essentials: food and shelter.

Step one accomplished.
On to the next rung!

Now that I had the security that I could provide the basics, the next step was to master a plan on how I would build another goose, a gosling of my own this time, one that I could nurture and grow myself and that I could be proud of.

It then occurred to me that I had been around someone for 20 years who had built a multimillion-dollar business from scratch. Every year, our life would get bigger and grander. I knew it meant growth, but never really paid attention to the big picture scope. I had a business mentor right by me for so many years. Post split, the distance allowed me to gain a new perspective on what I had experienced. I started to ask myself great questions: "How could I do like he did? How could I mimic what he built?" After all, my ex is not that big of a deal. Yes, he is a smart man, but he has a huge lazy streak and is not great at engaging people. Plus he lacks creativity and he is certainly very far from being an original. I have way more talent, gifts, and capacities than that… I confidently told myself if he could do it, I certainly could do it! I was ready to grow my own business. Entrepreneurship was the only way to go. Not only had I discovered how much I valued my time flexibility, but I also cared about building my own asset and found it important to remain in complete control of my money.

Producing an active income by means of rendering a product or a service to others meant that I needed to dig deep into me and find out who I really was. Integrity and Honesty are some of my top personal values, which meant that whatever I chose to do, it had to be in full alignment with my authentic self, with who I was at my core as well as be in accordance with my belief system. I am the kind of person who has to do something I passionately love otherwise I won't stick with it long term. I started to take a good look at myself from all possible angles. I decided to look at my gifts and pool my talents and observed what others turned to me for. I then combined the data and the reinvention process had begun.

I put it all in a pot and cooked up a new recipe that was to be me. I was now ready to embrace my true life purpose.

Eight years later, the fog has lifted and I can clearly see my path ahead. I am finally starting to live that fulfilled life I have been longing for. It is just the tip of the iceberg. I know I am just getting started. After downgrading my living for 6 years, I am finally moving to my first ever home, I feel more secure than ever in my financial road, and I am in a relationship where I am truly loved. Professionally, I have built a solid network of strong and dependable people. People who are committed to helping others as well as being dedicated to their own success. People who understand value, who understand people. People who stand for excellence of standards. Real people I could count on. A great community.
I trust that everything will work itself out in divine timing and that my only job is to be me! Life is growing slowly and it is bearing some of the sweetest fruits I could ever have imagined.

Paquita Varee Wright, SPHR, SHRM-SCP

Paquita Wright, SPHR, SHRM-SCP: Business owner, Human Resources Executive, coach, speaker and real estate investor. She came from humble beginnings as a child of a single teenager. With a loving and encouraging tell-it-like-it-is mom, "You can do anything! Be the boss...", Paquita's path would be very different than the one she witnessed.

She has been in the real estate arena for 26 years and shares her experiences through non-traditional real estate education. Paquita acquired her BA in Human Resources Management and for the last 20 years has focused on tying employee performance and satisfaction to the bottom line.

www.cpwrightassociates.com
www.flippmoney.com
www.paquitawright.com

Chapter 8

Pattern Interrupt

By Paquita Wright, SPHR, SHRM-SCP

My road to success started very early. It started with me observing patterns within my own family and then deciding I was going to create an entirely different one for myself.
It all began with home ownership…

The first house I ever wanted to buy was because my mother never owned her home until I was an adult. In fact, the majority of my family members were renters. The way my mother spoke of desiring home ownership, I was ready to have my name added to my first deed at 17. I got to the closing table and was told I had to wait two more weeks before signing. No one realized I was still a minor.

The next house I purchased was at 19, and my first one became a rental property. I was still in the military at the time but starting to realize something about myself that I'd heard from others all my life. People seemed to be attracted to me, sharing things with me not easily shared, accepting and seeking my feedback. Building and maintaining relationships with people came naturally to me. Equipped with this knowledge, and being pregnant, I knew I would not be in the military for long. So, being future focused, I thought about what I enjoyed and decided to pursue a career in real estate. Next step was getting my real estate license. With enough money saved to stay home with my baby for a year, I gave notice to the military that I would be separating to become a mom.

I grew up in the air capital of the world, Wichita, Kansas. It was a manufacturing city. It hosted plants for Cessna, Boeing, Spirit and other manufacturers of the sort. Most of my family members worked at a major hospital or at an air plant. Many of them weren't in any type of supervisory position. So, with any layoffs that happened it meant that immediately most of my family was unemployed.

I would hear stories growing up about how my mom or step dad or other family member was passed over for promotions, how they were being treated, about their work hours, and general complaints heard from most employees. While I learned great work ethics from my family of mostly the women who faithfully kept a job, most of their aspirations were to make more an hour than the job before.

I thank God for a mother who constantly praised me and made me want so much more.

PEEKING BEHIND THE SCENES

I've always been a planner with an insatiable drive to move forward and progress, and I really wasn't interested in starting from the bottom. My next logical step was to look up where in the U.S. could I be a real estate broker in the shortest amount of time possible. I was committed to working for myself. That said, I needed to start with some learning, and that was only going to happen by getting a job and 'doing'.

Once I got my real estate license, I was recruited by three companies: Century 21, Remax and this little company in Newport News, Virginia. What was interesting to me is that the owner of this small company said that if I was as smart as he thought I was, he was going to open up the books to me. That meant a lot to me, because it would allow me to see the back end of operations and I knew this is what I was working towards. I was completely honest and upfront with the owner, and I expressed my desire to one day open my own brokerage. He was true to his word and handed me over the reins, and even mentored me.

Within the year I was ready to move on. There were only two places in the U.S. where I could become a broker after just one year of being a real estate agent: Hawaii and Florida. Hawaii was a great idea, but the cost of living there was daunting. Florida was more affordable, and my husband had family in that State. So, Florida is where I got my broker's license.

Compiled by **JENNIFER LOW**

At 23/24 years old, I was the broker and the owner of a Century 21 franchise. I remember being in Parsippany, New Jersey for an owner's meeting... I walked into a room of people in their late 50s and late 60s. I was the youngest person there by a huge margin!

It was pretty amazing to be that young, but I didn't realize the significance of it then. I felt God had always shown me favor and the good things have always outweighed the bad. I have always been blessed, and I always knew where my blessings came from. I'm not the most religious person in the world, but I believe in God, and I believe in His higher power.

Being the owner of a real estate company, I had agents working for me, which gave me the opportunity to start doing different things rather than just resale. I started building homes, and within 5 years, I opened a second Century 21 franchise in a different location. By this time, I was 28 years old and had another baby on the way. Everything was going great. It was going so great that I was $12 away from having a million dollars **cash** in the bank.

Then one day, after having my vehicle serviced, my ride was bumpier than before. For whatever reason, someone had forgotten to tighten the lug nuts. While driving on the highway, one at a time, each tire came off! Needless to say, the consequences were quite dramatic: the vehicle flipped repeatedly, and I was ejected out.

PEEKING BEHIND THE SCENES

It was quite an experience. I was in the hospital for some time. After almost three years of therapy, shock treatment, speech therapy, occupational therapy, chiropractors, internal medicine doctors, I was almost as good as new… somewhat.

And this was where the real learning began.

By now, we had gone through all that cash in the bank. I had financially supported myself through my ordeal, I was supporting my husband who was at school, and I was also supporting my mom and my sister who were living with us at the time. The money got drained! I really didn't know anything about money, to begin with, because we really weren't a family that ever had money before. What I had learned is how to MAKE money. So without my ability to work and make the money, we were pretty much bankrupt. Within two years, I went from having a million dollars in the bank to one day writing an IOU for a pack of chicken legs. Unreal!

When I first opened my real estate company, I had a friend who was working HR (Human Resources). She would come to me often, because that people-person in me always shined through. When she was having different conflicts, she would come to me, and we'd talk about what she could do. I'd give her my perspective, and she would try it out. Her good results meant that she pulled me in on some consulting jobs with her company and I took to it very well. I continued consulting and took an HR job over the next few years after I sold my real estate business.

We then followed my husband to Georgia for his new job. I loved HR at the time, so I decided to get my bachelor's degree in Human Resources. While I was still in school, I applied for three jobs in HR. They were all director level positions or above. I remember my husband saying to me to just take anything so we can make ends meet. I knew I was capable and I was made for more. I had experience to speak of, and I stood my ground.

Out of the three positions, I applied for, I got an offer from two of them. I had to make a decision between going corporate for profit or corporate non-profit. I chose the latter as it was one of the largest non-profit organizations in Atlanta. When I got my first check, I don't remember if I quite laughed or cried. I guess it was somewhere in between. What I had made in that first pay check was so tiny to me, especially after owning my own company and being fed off of my own work as well as that of all my employees…

I was around 30/31 at the time. I was trying to come to grips with this when I suddenly realized I didn't need to come to grips with anything! I was not going to stay at that rate for long! So I wrote down a timeline of where I would be financially with this company in the months and years ahead. On paper, I had basically given myself a raise every 6 months.

I taped this paper on my credenza. Every turn I made in my chair, I could see it all the time. One day, the Chief Financial Officer whom I reported to, was in my office. While we were talking, it dawned on me that this note was in full view of her. Spotting it, she said to me, "kind of aggressive aren't we?" I made sure to tell her I had a higher power on my side.

Within my first 6 months, my salary was increased…twice! The CFO came to my office to find out how the increase compared to my 'projections'. I admitted my actual increase was more than I even knew to ask. Then, six months later I decided to ask for another increase. I walked out of the office with another $23 thousand tagged on to my annual pay.

Feeling confident, and, on the Board for some time now, which was something never offered to the previous head of HR, I was super loyal to the organization and turning down continuous offers by larger companies.

So, while I was still an employee, my title could have been anything, but it was understood I was a boss. My company standing, my pay, the benefits and the wonderful flexibility allowed me to get quite comfy and live a plush life. Unknowingly, I had become a slave to this life, and when I realized just how comfortable I had become I asked myself how I could start building and buying real estate again, on purpose rather than as a hobby.

At work, we had been through some mergers and there were a bunch of people who were laid off. Every time I was coming out pretty good, even getting a few more raises. Everything was looking good financially, but heart-wise, I felt things were changing. I was not being as authentic as I could be. I felt like my effectiveness was changing and it was starting to change my view of my inner self. Things were changing within the company and decisions I didn't like were starting to make me question ME. It was becoming more about business and bottom line regardless of the moral or literal costs. It was then that I asked myself: "If I didn't have this job tomorrow, what would it mean for me and my family?" It was devastating to look at the answer. I certainly didn't want to relive my previous financial post-accident experience.

I had to do something different, because I was aware that anything could happen at any time!

In October 2013, I attended a seminar called the Millionaire Mind Intensive, in Atlanta. By taking part in higher-level courses and associating with its community, I was extremely motivated to break free and be me. Without the training and the relationships, never would I have been okay with walking away from $200,000 dollars annually. The job was stealing my life, my time with my kids and my soul. Being a part of this new community allowed me the security and confidence for what I needed to do next. "My" plan allowed for a slow and steady transition into my next phase. So I started my HR firm two years before I left my job.

When the CEO of the company I was working for was thinking of retiring, I wanted to be walking out the door with her. After a brief chat with her regarding my double exit plan, I decided to stay on for a little longer. I was to make sure the change was going to happen smoothly for everyone. It was around that time that I also found out I was pregnant. Chaos was happening, but it was a natural point of transition for me to let go of that job. The nudge of the incoming leadership sealed the deal.

I now have my consulting firm in HR, *CPWright and Associates* that is up, going, and growing. Everything is in place to bid and work on government projects although most of my work still comes from word of mouth. This time I am constantly working my business towards complete systemization. So, I am working on the transition into a self-sufficient business instead of another job for me where I just happen to own the company.

I also have my real estate company, *FlippMoney*, a solid investing program with an educational twist. The magic of reclaiming my life is to figure out ways to systematize what I love doing so that my businesses can run without me. I provide education on how to make your money work for you in real estate while remaining accessible for the ones who want more guidance.

These two businesses coupled with my success in building passive income are providing the baseline of my current lifestyle while pushing me towards my desired lifestyle.

Before I wrap this up let me say, for those seeking success, I hope that in my few pages, the reader gets these few things. 1. Know what you want (and don't want) so you can keep your eyes on the prize. 2. Write it down and remind yourself often. 3. Always bounce back and 4. Believe in something… so that when life kicks yo' ass, and it will, you have something to pull you back up inside. Also know that these things were possible because of some late nights, early mornings, hearing lots of NOs, recovering quickly, cleaning toilets at night with a Board meeting in the morning and so many more sacrifices.

How bad do you want it?

PEEKING BEHIND THE SCENES

There is a term in NLP called Pattern Interrupt. It's when you create confusion in your mind to be able to reset your thinking while disposing of old patterns that were usually set in by other influences in your life and to create new patterns that will serve you better. Perhaps my whole life up to now has been a pattern interrupt... and now I am finally living the way that I want to!

I love my life!

Arlene Pe Benito

Arlene engages with her clients to mentor and empower those who find themselves stuck in the same patterns over and over. Through a simple process and a holistic approach, the root of the pattern is revealed and then transformed through several areas of their life: relationships, health and wealth. Arlene is a results-based coach, guaranteeing your results in writing.

Arlene is a Master Reiki Practitioner, Certified Master Teacher in Magnified Healing, Certified Master Neuro Linguistic Practitioner, Certified Master NLP Coach, Certified Master Time Line Therapist, Certified Master Hypnotherapist and Certified Trainer of Hypnotherapy, designated in over 38 countries.

You can contact Arlene via:

Email:livingwithcolour.coach@gmail.com
Website: www.livingwithcolour.coach
Facebook: www.facebook.com/arlene.p.benito

Chapter 9

A Peek Behind the Scenes to my Deliberate Path

By Arlene Pe Benito

What is success? It can mean so many things to so many people. Growing up, success to me meant power and money. Now as an entrepreneur, yes, money is great, but success is so much more than that. To me, success is defined as finding my life purpose and putting it into action by helping others to know that it is safe to speak their truth! I thereby leave an enduring legacy, knowing that I made a difference in the community.

As I sit here writing a chapter for my first published piece, I'm thinking to myself: "WOW, I am blessed!" Not many people have these opportunities just handed to them, let alone, have the guts to take them.

How did I get here? Let me tell you it wasn't easy. Actually, it was quite messy. In fact, less than 6 months ago, I was working a corporate job and was on the management team. I was on 'special projects' and making a name for myself within the corporation. This was a place I called home for over 10 years. I was paid well, and I was damn good at my job!

At work, I was known as the person who was positive and happy, and who "made people smile." I was a balance of wit and fun, mixed with the perfect amount of leadership qualities that got people to do what they had to do to make the entire team successful. Aside from the usual hustle and bustle of the everyday things, I had no complaints.

After several situations at work where I felt like I was being mistreated, I finally got the courage to stick up for myself. After days of thinking and worrying, I decided to speak to a leader and ask for help. In doing so, it triggered such a profound sequence of events that I was left reeling. Word spread like wildfire, and I quickly became segregated from the group. To make matters worse, I felt I was being punished by having projects taken away from me as well as other changes to my work responsibilities. I had finally harnessed the guts to speak my truth, and it did not work out in my favour.

In such a short period of time my world had toppled over, and as most of the structures in my life crashed down, my mask came off with it, leaving me vulnerable and in pain. 'The Corporation' was my identity. My colleagues were my family. I spent so much time thinking: how could they do this to me? I had spent hours upon hours at work, going in early and leaving late on my own accord so that everything would be perfect and ready. I had been committed to my corporate success for years. If I wasn't at work an hour and half early, I considered myself late and felt stressed and guilty. I spent an hour or two with my children every day, and for the most part, I was okay with that because I justified it with being successful, and being successful for me at that time, meant providing for my girls even if it wasn't with my time. At work I was happy go lucky. In contrast, I was spent by the time I got home. The consequence of this was that with my family, friends and especially my children, I was angry and impatient.

I was 'Living the Life' that I thought I deserved. My goal was to work in one place until retirement, and receive that wonderful 'pension' which came with a 30 year anniversary gold watch. And boy was I working extra hard to achieve it.

Day by day I watched, as things would progressively worsen. Projects were gone, the trust of employees and colleagues was so easily tarnished, and I walked through the motions of my day. I found myself crying as I walked along the work floor while I watched people whispering about me. I was embarrassed and ashamed. Unable to sleep, unable to eat, I did my best to continue going through the motions and presenting myself as a strong working woman. Finally, I was encouraged to go see my family physician.

Before she even had a chance to sit down in her chair, I broke down in tears and was hyperventilating as I told her my story. Heartbroken, I gave her detail after detail. I was an absolute mess.

I remember as my Doctor, and I went through the checklist…
"Are you eating?" "No."
"Are you sleeping?" Sniffle, "No."
"Are you having thoughts of death"… etc

Upon completion of the checklist, my physician told me that I was severely depressed. She suggested some antidepressants and informed me that I needed some time off from work, so that I could heal. I remember looking at her incredulously, and saying, "Are you crazy? I have to work! This is my job!" Soothingly she looked back at me and asked me if I realized that it was work that was causing me to be sick, and that the easiest way to heal from this was by being away from it for a short time. I finally agreed to take some time for myself.

Time for myself… what the hell did that mean?

Looking back, it was the hardest and most painful experience I have ever had to endure so far. My body was racked with pain. My head… daily it wanted to explode. My mind… at the time it couldn't even function to do my daily activities. I wasn't sleeping, I wasn't eating. There were days I could not even get out of bed to care for my children and bring them to school. Thank goodness I lived with family. I disconnected from everyone, including myself. The people around me couldn't understand that I wasn't well. On the outside everything looked the same, but I knew there was something different and I wasn't snapping out of it. My colleagues were texting me, that at work, there were hints that I was 'faking it' to get time off. I started to ask myself: "How does one prove that one has a mental illness?"

By telling my story to myself day in and day out, and to anyone that would listen, I lived my story with such commitment and conviction that I got exactly what I asked for: overnight, I developed a severe facial twitch. My face would contort over and over again. It was aggressive and painful. I had manifested it into my life so I had a way to show people that I was ill. Some called me crazy, because there was no other way to react when they saw me. My children thought it was hilarious, and it became a joke with them. This led me further into hiding.

As a Master Reiki Practitioner, I had tools that I could use. Reiki is a wonderful healing modality that channels energy into the body. In order for the intelligent energy to flow through my body, I have no choice but to connect with my body.

Healing myself and removing the layers of masks that I had been wearing for years led me to a crossroads in my career path. Do I stay or do I go? The corporation that I was part of for a decade, no longer filled my cup. In fact, I allowed it to empty it. I allowed myself to become so dependent on a business that wasn't mine and engross it into my identity, that only small parts of the real me peeked through. Daily, I woke up thinking, "Who am I and how the hell did I get here?"

Weekly, I would see a therapist. And though I honored her work, it was a weekly repetition of the pain that I had gone through. After months of seeing her, I was feeling anxiety on my drive to see her. I finally decided enough was enough. I needed to change something. Opening up the wounds on a weekly basis while expecting a different result was not logical! I started my new path by asking myself one question: "Who do I want to become?"

I wanted to be me! Authentically me!

In that moment, I decided, I could no longer return to that same work environment. I was going to leave a working community that disempowered me, and that did not create a healthy atmosphere for me. I made the decision to step into my own power, and take whatever power back that I had given away. It was time to start climbing up and out of this deep dark hole I had been sitting in.

PEEKING BEHIND THE SCENES

To my surprise, opportunities came forward. Within weeks, I was presented with a beautiful gift of free branding, and support in creating a website from two friends in the advertising industry. They were looking to give back by empowering and supporting women entrepreneurs. These women in turn, introduced me to a beautiful soul. This financial advisor who supported and walked me through my financial details, helped me move forward in starting my business and putting a support structure in place to create the life that I wanted. This beautiful soul introduced me to another amazing woman, a twelve time international best seller, whom after meeting wanted me to be a part of a project with her! This international bestselling author, introduced me to another author, which led me to be published for the first time. How absolutely honoring is that?

With so many parts of my life coming together, I knew I had to take further action. As such, I made an appointment with a multifaceted energy healer outside of my community to provide me with other holistic modalities and insights. She gave me a list of tasks and I worked hard to complete them. This was integral in my healing. Committing to myself was important. Gaining the trust of self was imperative. The gift of this commitment resulted in flow. I was in the flow. Things were coming with ease, and that's how life was meant to be. Working with this angel led me to other modalities of healing.

I knew that this would be the turning point of what I needed and only add to my journey.

The most important thing that I have learned is that to be wealthy, healthy and happy, one needs to take action. Action is made up of three things, which are all integral in creating a change in your life. To take action, one must spend: Time, Energy and Money. First, commit to spending time on yourself to make a change. Secondly, use your own energy to create the change. Lastly, invest in yourself, and it will lead you to change.

I am a case in point!

In the months that followed my decision to step fully into creating a sustainable business for myself, I made sure to use this formula. It transformed me and transformed my life by shifting my perspectives through learning, and healing. Within a short amount of time, I have become a Master Teacher in Magnified Healing, Master Neuro Linguistic Practitioner, Master NLP Coach, Master Time Line Therapist, Master Hypnotherapist and Trainer of Hypnotherapy. I am designated in over 38 countries. I am a results-based coach, and I can guarantee your results in writing.

All healing modalities work, and in my own experience, each has a place in sequence. The modalities listed above work cohesively together. In my own experiences and observing the experiences of so many others, I learned that healing does not have to be hard and painful. In fact, it can be quite the opposite.

Another tool that I incorporate into my everyday life and teach others is the question: "Does this bring me closer or further away from my goal?" Answering this question leads you to your 'why'. Your WHY is the first and foremost statement to start from. Many of us, myself included, get stuck in the HOW and WHAT. Hows and whats lead us to the workings of life, and the spinning out of control. It is from here that we find it a challenge to make a decision on something, not realizing that it may lead us to illness, to being stuck, and to have that feeling of being out of control. But, if you focus on your WHY, you will know your goal and choose your steps accordingly.

This year has led me to my why. Why am I doing what I'm doing? Why did I leave the comfy cozy corporate job to pursue my own business? Why did I move forward in my learning and development? Why did I continue my healing journey?

I did it for me. I did it because I am here to empower, inspire and engage with others. I am here to support people on a healing journey through self discovery. Life afforded me some great challenges, and here I am today without regret, for they led me to who I am right now. I am here because it is safe to speak my truth. I am proof that you can be the person you want to be. You are the creator of your own life. And if you are reading this and feel a spark or some intrigue, then perhaps it is time to pay attention. Pain in any way, shape, or form means you must pay attention. What is happening in your life right now, that is saying: "Look at me!! You're avoiding something! There's something to look at here. Pay attention!"

Life is not hard. Each of our lives is meant to naturally flow like water in a riverbed. If you are not flowing, then what is it that is holding you back from investing yourself fully into your dream and into your vision? We each have one life to lead. We create every moment of it and we have choice in every moment as well. Life sends us little hints and signs, and when we don't listen they get amplified. We all deserve 100% from life. We deserve to have everything we've ever wanted. Why not choose to lead your life, rather than letting life lead you? It will take you places you never knew existed, and I'm happy and proud to say that I am proof of that.

Success is such a personal word. And when speaking of it, it's what provides me with the most joy, happiness, and vibrant life. I am successful because I am empowering, inspiring and engaging with others while using these tools. And this answers my why! I am wealthy, healthy and happy. Wouldn't it be wonderful to learn how you can too? How can you not take the opportunity?

Holly A. Kline

Holly Kline is a published author and motivational speaker who has overcome many of life's difficulties, trials and tribulations. She is the author of *7 Times Saved*, which describes her seven near-death experiences, her passion for life, and her message of perseverance to reach personal success. She thereby inspires people to discover their own inner strength and willpower to "Keep Moving Forward" and in the process, brings hope to others. Holly presently resides in Ottawa, Canada with her grandson Gordon, of whom she has legal guardianship.

hollyklineauthor@gmail.com
www.linkedin.com/in/holly-a-kline-author
www.facebook.com.holly.kline.393

Chapter 10

Keep Moving Forward

By Holly A. Kline

In March 2002, I found myself in the Ottawa Civic Hospital for an entire month after the cable of an elevator broke. I had fallen six and half floors, plunging 65 feet at 125km/h, while in the elevator box.

After a week in the emergency room, I had been laying on the gurney, when a nurse said she saw me moving my leg with the rest of my body and accused me of faking my paralysis. I was appalled. Who in their right mind would want to be here? All my big life prayers had been answered: my hopes and dreams of having a loving family, a government job, and a beautiful semi-detached home in the suburbs— it had all been accomplished. I had everything that I could only have dreamed of as a child. Why would I wish this upon myself? I certainly didn't want to be here!

By the end of the week, the Rehab Specialist came over to visit me. He diagnosed my right leg as being paralyzed. The doctor ordered the ambulance crew to prepare me for transportation to the Rehab Hospital. He told me to embrace this change in my life, as my new condition could range from months to years.

I began crying. My life as I knew it was over.
The ambulance crew boarded me into the back of their truck to get me to the Rehab Centre. During my ride, I prayed for the Universe to release me from my present burdens of being paralyzed. I wondered why I was still alive.

My mind drifted…

I began to remember hearing a story on the radio about a guy who had fallen from a couple of floors at his construction job and became paralyzed. He had two young sons, a wife, and a beautiful home. Shortly after his accident, he committed suicide. Apparently he did not want to become a burden on his family. I began to wonder if I would also become a burden on mine.

I also remembered…

In 1966, my Dad left our family shortly before my twin and I were born. He returned home from his peacekeeping mission in Cyprus when I was 6 months old. Upon arriving home, he discovered that mom had allowed a new man to move into our house, and as a result, Dad left shortly after. Mom was left to raise five young children on her own.

PEEKING BEHIND THE SCENES

When my older siblings moved out, Mom's resentment and abusive temper grew towards my sister and me. One night, she lost her temper badly. She dragged me from the top bunk and into the kitchen. She beat me so badly I stopped trying to protect myself and started to lose my zest for life. I hoped that she would stop and allow me to go back to bed. I could lie in my bed and die in peace. The years of torture, beatings and lost hope had taken a toll on me, and I didn't care anymore. Finally, when she noticed that I had given up the fight, she ordered me to go back to bed.

Crawling to my pillow on my bed, I began to pray. I wondered about my self-worth, what purpose I had in this life and why I was still here. Although I was always a fighter and pushed through everything that came my way, I somehow knew that I had a deeper purpose. I was already beating the odds.

I remembered…

In August 1984, my stepsisters and I headed to the beach for a swim. The water was too choppy to swim safely, but the peer pressure got to me and I went in anyways. As I swam in deep water with white caps splashing in my face, I began to swallow water and was having difficulty breathing. I realized that if I had listened to my gut feeling and paid attention to all the warning signs, I could have prevented my current situation completely. The water continued to splash over my head. My lungs felt as though they could explode with the pressure of the water. I began sinking to the bottom of the lake, and felt myself fading in and out of consciousness. I was terrified. I stretched out my hand in hopes that somebody might catch it. Just at the cusp between life and death, I felt somebody touch the tip of my hand, and drag me to shore. I was placed into the recovery position and felt very grateful to be alive.

I remembered…

On December 9th, 1988 my second daughter was born with complications. The cord was around her throat, cutting off her blood supply. The doctors ordered me to stop pushing as the pressure was cutting off her air and when I did, the pressure inadvertently travelled to my heart and stopped it. I woke up to a nurse vigorously rubbing two defibrillator pads.
"What are you doing?" I asked the nurse. She replied, "You already flat-lined twice, and it looks like you're going again. I want to make sure that you don't, especially since I really had to fight to bring you back the second time."

I remembered…
In November 1989, I was 22 years old, and expecting my third child. My husband and I were living in a cramped one-bedroom apartment. I started working as a full-time overnight

cashier in a neighborhood convenience store, while attending adult night school to obtain my grade 12 English. As a result, the Children's Aid Society (CAS) stepped in to offer some respite assistance.

In February 1990, my husband was fired from his full-time job and we had to move out of Ottawa. Before our necessary move, we decided to use the money from his severance package for our long overdue honeymoon: a ten-day road trip to Phoenix, Arizona. My sister agreed to take care of our children in her home in London, Ontario, while we were away.

Our trip went very well, until our drive home, when we hit black ice during a freak winter storm in the southern part of the US. Our car's rear end flipped over its hood and then rolled two and a half times on its side and landed on its roof. Our only witness, a transport truck driver, called the authorities immediately and made mention that it was a miracle that we were still alive!

The next day, we were safely back home in Ottawa. I called my sister only to find out that she had given up my kids to the CAS. The girls were in foster care awaiting a permanent placement, unless I was to show up in London, at the CAS office by 9:00 am on Monday morning to fight for them.

My heart sank to the pit of my stomach. I was in shock and in disbelief.

I arrived in London late Sunday. My brother picked me up at the Greyhound bus station and took me to his home for the night. Early the next day, I went to the Courthouse before 9:00 am to dispute my case. Within a few minutes, the CAS in London found out about my case in Ottawa, and requested a short recess to call their office. When we reconvened they stated that they found favorable results. My file was closed. I was granted permission to see my children right away, and to take them home within three days.

I remembered…
In October 1990, as a divorced single mother of three, I spent my days with my children. One night, at about 10 pm, I awoke to a crying baby and rain entering my unit through the open window. After closing the window, feeding her and laying her back down to sleep, I began drying up the water. I also heard a loud thumping noise and remembered that I had left the basement window open above the washing machine. I headed downstairs. When I reached the basement, I pulled the washing machine plug out of its socket while standing in half a foot of water and was instantly hit with 23 amps of electricity. I knew I should have let go of the plug, but my hand was glued to it. I woke up in the spot where I had landed with a thud several feet away from the machine. It

seemed like only moments later, yet when I checked the clock, hours had already slipped by. I made my way up two flights of stairs slowly passing my daughters as they slept in their beds. I was grateful I wasn't unconscious any longer than I had been, thankful that I had survived and that my children were safe.

I remembered...

In 2012 I was diagnosed with Post Traumatic Stress Disorder (PTSD). Having served for my country and now a veteran, I was severely depressed and was hospitalized for a week. It was around that time I lost my entire family. They all decided to move away. My youngest moved to Florida, my eldest and her daughter went to the Netherlands, and my other daughter was fighting me in court for the custody of her child. It was not a good year.

The battle included defending myself from the tough childhood I had had, and what I had accomplished on my own. The CAS wondered how they could possibly hand over permanent custody of a child they had in their care knowing how I had been brought up in a criminal family. But no matter what was thrown at me I kept moving forward. I wasn't prepared to let any of my family history hold me back. I could have easily told myself so many times while I was growing up that "I'm in this crap and this is where I'm going to stay".

Instead, I pushed through, I moved forward. I had graduated from college when I wasn't even expected to finish high school. I had survived beatings and drowning and much worse. I had successfully obtained my dream job when I worked for and with the RCMP for two and a half years, even if it was just as a civilian. I had pride! I had successfully broken my family's patterns. I was committed to never be like them. I was persistent to live differently than my immediate family, differently than the experiences I had growing up, and despite it all, I had been determined to find my purpose.

Suddenly…

I was brought back to the present situation. We had arrived at the Rehab Hospital. I felt the tension in my back release, I was no longer cramped in one position, and I felt the sensation in my leg return. By the time the paramedics parked in front of the Rehab Centre, I had unbuckled my seatbelt on the gurney, and I was standing inside the ambulance. The ambulance crew was amazed. They looked at each other in shock and said: "This is a miracle. You were paralyzed and now you are walking." I asked them if they wouldn't mind helping me down from the back of the ambulance. I was re-examined and then discharged. I had once again been given another chance.
I had withstood all sorts of life and near-death challenges, and by the grace of God I was still here, I was still standing. I was not going to allow this accident to hinder me, just like I hadn't

allowed any of my previous ones to stand in my way. I had experienced much worse. I still had a lot of life in me to give. Somehow, I knew that there was more for me to do.

Although I was no longer paralyzed, my physical fight had just begun. Over the next few years, my body went through a considerable ordeal to recover further from that elevator incident. As I continued my rehab at home surrounded by my loving family, I felt supported and stronger for it. My children and I have now been reunited and we have a stronger bond than ever before. I see my grandchildren daily, after school and for family dinners. I also gained full custody and guardianship of my grandson Gordon. And I continue to pray and I always remember to be thankful for another day.

I now share my stories through writing and speaking. I love to help others see the positive in anything that is served to them in their life. A positive outlook is a big key to having a successful life. I know I have encouraged others to look past the obstacles they are currently facing and I have inspired them to start succeeding.

Because let's face it: if I can do it, you can too!

Jane "Trainer Jane" Warr

Jane "Trainer Jane" Warr is a Communications or Relationship Coach, delivering life-transforming experiential educational programs, which combine advanced communications skills and emotional intelligence.

Further, as a Business Coach, Jane delivers powerful seminars and workshops, as well as works with clients one-on-one, and in groups. Her unique "Selling on the Spot Marketplace" events are held all across Southern Ontario.

Jane sits on the Board of Directors of StartUp Durham, is also an International Best-Selling Published Author, a Real Estate Investor, and the proud mom of two young adults.
She has been on tv, in magazines, and interviewed for books and radio.

www.TrainerJaneSays.com
www.facebook.com/TrainerJane
www.Linkedin.com/in/janewarr

Chapter 11

Pivots

By Jane "Trainer Jane" Warr

I have been an entrepreneur most of my life. Perhaps that was originally because I am an introvert, and it certainly was because I loved the freedom of setting my own hours, choosing how I employ myself, and controlling my own destiny.

After being a stay at home mom for many years, I found myself in the position of wanting, and needing, to reinvent myself, and to earn an income. I had no interest in having a "job" or being employed by someone else, and being outside of my home for that matter. I had to do some soul searching to discover what I was most passionate about.

Knowing that I wanted to help people, work with individuals and that I was passionate about fitness, health, wellness and self-care, I pursued an education to become a Personal Trainer. My journey in fitness began with me surprising myself by choosing to work for a large company in a gym. I loved the people, enjoyed the atmosphere, as well as my personal growth. I worked my way up quickly to a Fitness Manager position, only to decide that, although I could do the work and enjoyed it to a degree, I felt working in a small office was not for me. Quickly I realized I couldn't do that long term, certainly not with the enthusiasm and zest for life I wanted to feel daily.

As soon as I became self-employed again, I named my business "Trainer Jane", and labeled myself a Personal Trainer and Nutrition Coach. I had the freedom to make all my decisions again and knew I wanted to follow the demand of my clients, and that of the marketplace, and add coaching to my services. The addition was a natural fit for my clients, for them to get a more well-rounded, balanced package of fitness AND nutrition coaching. They were asking me for nutrition tips and advice regularly, so I thought, "Why not monetize what I was already doing?" That was an early pivot in my business.

Soon after, I started studying more about entrepreneurship, and the many roles that need to be filled, especially as a solo-preneur. The main roles are those of the Visionary, the Manager, and the Implementer. We naturally are best at one, weakest at one, with the third somewhere in between. I am definitely a Visionary first, an Implementer second, and a Manager third. Know your strengths and weaknesses. Work your strengths and know when to delegate and hire out your weaknesses. Let others fill the roles that they can do better and faster than you. Look at it from a business investment position. It was a better investment for me to pay someone for two hours than try to do it myself in five. The end result from them was better quality too because it was their skill set and their passion.

I also hired a coach, and later a second and third coach, to aid with different segments of my business, and pull me further along. Building this team around me, helped me see much more for me, for "Trainer Jane" the business, and for my clients. My vision for myself expanded tremendously. I believe in thinking BIG and dreaming BIG!

"Your playing small does not serve the world."
- *Marianne Williamson*

Another pivot came when I was introduced to a communications course called Verbal Aikido. It is a life-transforming, one of a kind workshop and home study course, that combines advanced communications skills, emotional intelligence, and the powerful non-adversarial philosophy of the Japanese martial art, Aikido.

Not only did it transform some of my important personal relationships, but it also helped heal some past emotional hurts in the process. "Everyone wants to feel heard, understood, accepted, and respected." was one of many valuable lessons for me.

In regards to my business, Verbal Aikido helped me focus, instead of procrastinate, thereby increasing my productivity. It gave me the skills towards conflict resolution, to learn and master assertiveness, and of course increase revenue.

Learning to "Control Self, Manage Interactions, and Influence Others" is indeed vital to all communication demands on a daily basis.

When offered to partner, as a licensed facilitator, with James MacNeil, the author and founder of Verbal Aikido, it seemed a no-brainer for me. I was passionate about bringing it to the public and wanted to pursue taking it to companies and corporations too. I had no problem with the idea of monetizing it. I knew my worth and the value I provided.

I understood the difference between pursuing a "passion project" and a "profit project". I knew Verbal Aikido for the public was a passion project for me. It fed my soul! Verbal Aikido for companies was a profit project, with higher pay potential per speech.

Since I was putting on local presentations for the public, especially to stir up interest in Verbal Aikido and help with its branding, I formally added the title "Speaker" to my bio. Pivot!

By now I had embraced my pivots as not just change, but significant advancements in my career! I was a "Public Figure"!

Soon after, I was asked to collaborate on a writing project. I proudly coauthored the book: *Manifesting a New Life: Money, Love, Health and Everything in Between*. It became an International Best Seller the first day on the market! It felt cathartic writing my chapter for that book, and it helped me reflect and appreciate the journey I had been on thus far as Trainer Jane, as well as my personal and professional growth. I laughed often explaining the difference between being an author and a writer. I didn't think I was a talented writer, but I had now authored a book. I was now considered an authority on another subject. I could not only say I was a Published Author, but of an International Best Seller! Wow! Pivot.

I had learned to seek strategic partnerships. Who did I want to partner with and what was the desired outcome? I was building myself to be an authority in my field. Getting published was seen as a great accomplishment, and built up my credibility and visibility.

Feeding my desire to create, teach, coach, improve and build, I held an event I strategically created before the Christmas holiday season, called "Selling on the Spot Marketplace". My goal was to gather like-minded entrepreneurs and get them to not just network, but *sell* each other their products and services. Why not "Ask for the Sale!" after getting to know someone, and explaining to them what you do?

This concept took off like a wildfire! It has now been successfully running in my area where it all started and has been travelling around Southern Ontario, by demand!

A sense of community and positivity had been created by gathering men and women together at varying stages of their entrepreneurial journeys. They came from any and every business type and sought to collaborate and partner. I revelled hearing of their results through my events!

Why were people telling their friends about it? Through this event I was teaching "Ethical Selling, " and entrepreneurs found it to be a new and refreshing concept to learn, they were getting out of their comfort zone and trying new ways to communicate about their business, while they were having fun and selling!

Cash flow is crucial for any business, especially when new and growing. Sales is something to master. Sales shouldn't be considered negative, or dreaded; it is the lifeblood of your business. Love your business, speak about it passionately, and sell yourself. Love what you do, as I do.

Events became such a big part of my business model by this point that I knew if I wanted to increase my cash flow in my business, I could plan and market another event, sell tickets to it, and sell other services there too. This helped build my marketing funnel.

With organizing and running these events, I was labeled a Business Coach, and entrepreneurs were coming to me for help in growing themselves and their businesses. I was only a few years ahead of them, yet they were watching my quick public growth in business and wanted the same. I was no master of social media, but knew what I wanted to convey in my messaging, and it worked.

I had a brand strategy, having researched and created my business vision, my mission statement, and my core values list. I revisited them periodically and practised what I preached.

During this extreme growth process, a very valuable lesson was brought to my attention about being too humble. When publicly speaking or introducing myself, I understated or left out accomplishments to not seem the braggart. Over and over, individuals in my audience would come to me after to ask me to speak *more* about my journey. They wanted to know the details. They wanted to hear the successes. They loved and appreciated the inspiration it provided them.

A great way for me to realize how far I had come, was when I was asked to sit on the Board of Directors for an entrepreneurial organization. I felt like I had "made it". This was validation. I was honoured to just have been considered! Realizing the personal and business growth potential for me, I didn't hesitate to say yes! I was part of a team of entrepreneurs that I felt were more successful than me and knew my status had elevated again. Pivot!

Proudly, I sit on the Leadership Team of StartUp Durham, a chapter of StartUp Canada, in the roles of Communications Training, Sales Training, and Event Promotions and Management.

I have said yes to many opportunities that have come my way, and have been strategic about them. There have been good days and bad days. I have been challenged, I have been tested, and I have persevered!

I remind myself daily to practice what I preach, going back all the way to my fitness and nutrition background. I remind myself to take care of myself first, as only then can I lead

PEEKING BEHIND THE SCENES

through business. That is a piece of the legacy I want to leave behind. I constantly work on work/life balance, and guard self care time. I know my limits and don't test my health!

I have never worked harder in my life. I have never been happier in my life. I embrace my "good problems" as learning lessons that are needed at the time towards my personal and business growth and know that I didn't come this far, only to come this far.

I am grateful for every experience and person that has been a part of the journey thus far. I love to serve and am honoured to be in these roles.

Like most entrepreneurs, I am not satisfied with just these achievements. I want more, faster. I have a greater vision for my business, and serving more is what gets me up in the morning and drives me. Now I have a team of consultants that I work with. Work smarter, not harder!

The services I now provide, as "Trainer Jane", fall under the umbrella of Coaching. To the public and to businesses, I am now known as a Verbal Aikido Communications Coach. By doing this, I know I am transforming lives both personally and professionally. I also am a Business Coach, specializing in Entrepreneurial Success. I coach not only one-on-one but provide group coaching in person and online. The group coaching is a monthly recurring income stream. Selling on the Spot Marketplace has grown in its first year into a Southern Ontario-wide event experience that is now morphing into potential licensing deals!

Next year may look like more of the same for me in others' eyes, but it will be on a grander scale. I know there will be tremendous exponential growth in this for me. Perhaps there will be another pivot. I look forward to finding out!

PEEKING BEHIND THE SCENES

Holly Porter

Holly Porter is the Image Master and founder of The Image Designers. Holly is an International Speaker who inspires business breakthroughs and personal transformations. She is an Author, Coach, Hypnotist, Cosmetologist, Master Esthetician and Instructor/Educator. With over 30 years in Beauty and Business Industry, Holly understands what it takes to be successful in business, life, and can help YOU achieve success and abundance.

Holly has a gift for working with people. She is a listener, a problem solver, and she puts her whole heart into her work.

See her at **www.HollyPorter.com,**
https://www.facebook.com/theimagedesigners
or Set up your complimentary session today at
www.callwithHolly.com

Chapter 12

I Am Enough

By Holly Porter

I get a lot of my inspiration from songs. As I was thinking about writing this chapter and what I would like to share with you, this Kenny Rogers' song came to me. It's called *The Gambler,* and it goes like this.

You've got to know when to hold 'em
Know when to fold 'em
Know when to walk away
And know when to run
You never count your money
When you're sittin' at the table
There'll be time enough for countin'
When the dealin's done

To me, this says a lot about success. It's all about taking risks. Have you ever heard the risk takers are the moneymakers? A lot of it has to do with our personality: what we are willing to risk, how much we are willing to sacrifice, what we are willing to give and how much we are willing to take. I have always been a risk taker. In business, in relationships, and with other important decisions. I have never been sorry for it. Maybe it hasn't always served me, and at the same time, I would not change the decisions I have made. The "not so good" choices have been where I have grown the most spiritually and mentally.

We are all unique in our design, in who we are. We all have gifts that if we do not use, we will lose. Some of us have many gifts. Some of us use them for good, and some of us do not appreciate them.

One of the biggest lessons I have learned in my life is to listen for discernment, that inspiration that helps me make the best choice.

No, I have not always made the best choices, and I have simply learned from those moments. I am grateful every day for each lesson that I have learned, because it has made me into the person I am today.

I grew up as a redheaded freckle faced, four-eyed girl with the last name McDonald. Growing up, I felt like I had it pretty rough. I was bullied, teased and made fun of. Some of my childhood memories consist mostly of me crying every day. I had these two friends I thought were my besties from age 5 to 14. We all lived 3 houses from each other and attended the same school and the same class until the sixth grade. They were mean to me 80% of the time. They would call me names and throw rocks at me while walking home from school. The other 20% of the time they were fighting between themselves. Then I could pick which one to play with and have one of them all to myself. This set me up for a whole life of the same thing!

I grew up in Las Vegas and moved to Utah when I was 14. I moved to a city called New Harmony. Population: 198! I had to take the bus to school 25 miles away. The schools in Utah were behind Nevada academically. I had the choice to skip to the 9th grade if I wanted to, but I decided to stay back in the eighth grade mostly because of the fear of High School itself. I graduated as a Junior. Not because I was so smart, I just didn't really care for the structure of school. I know now that I have some dyslexia and ADHD and that was only discovered in my late 30-40s. Being that I was so active, it was hard to focus. I was a born leader, and yet I had let others influence so much of my life. I was gullible, naive and wanted everyone to be happy and get along!

I always hung out with the "older kids" and was mature for my age. My ambition then was to work three jobs, get married and have a perfect family! Be careful what you wish for. I have always had three jobs, by choice. After I graduated, I married my first husband that next year. It was an abusive relationship that I endured for 7 years and walked away with my three awesome children. Next, I married a playboy. We should have just stayed friends. Then my youngest gift was born from that marriage. I had married an older man who didn't understand I wasn't his sugar mama. By this time of my life, I had four great kids, my own home, my own business and a car. If I couldn't find someone who could give me more than the real true love that I deserved, then single I would stay.

Along came my husband, Scott. He is about as perfect as they come. This one was a keeper. We have been married almost 15 years to date. He listens and supports ALL my ambitions and desires. We have raised 8 children, and at this time we have 8 grandchildren.

Despite my wonderful family at the time, I had discovered that I was allowing myself to be influenced by what others thought of me. I was in my 30's before I realized I was doing this, and I was well into my 40's before I knew how to change it. I was making sure, unknowingly, in some way that other people were defining who I was instead of taking charge of that myself.

One day, I said "No! I will no longer put up with this. ENOUGH! These people will NOT define me. I am a daughter of God, and I have a purpose." At times I didn't know what that purpose was; I just knew I had one.

PEEKING BEHIND THE SCENES

People were meant to be happy. No one should live in fear of what others think, say or do to define them... NO ONE! I have the right to be myself! I had spent quite some time defending the underdogs why didn't I defend myself?

I've always loved the story of the ugly duckling. I feel that everyone deserves another chance or a 'do-over'. Just because I was made to feel 'ugly' did not mean that I was. It was more important for me to be a complete package: beautiful on the inside as well as the outside.

Personal development was always very important to me. Learning, growing, and finding out new ways to do things have been my passion.

It has taken a lot of years to get to this place in my life, where I feel content and satisfied with who I am. Of course, I'm not as perfect as I'd like to be; I wake up to more gray hairs every day, my textured skin will never be smooth and soft like in my younger years, but I have learned to accept those imperfections and just BE! My physical being is not the complete package by any means.

A big defining moment in my life was when I was running for political office. Those were exciting days, full of new experiences, and yet those were also the days that brought me to a very dark place within. There is way too much juice to this story to share here, but I will tell you that it was a most necessary life lesson. In fact, it was one of my biggest life lessons to date. To be completely honest, it was harder than failing at three marriages.

I ran for office three times. Two of those were for City Council and one time was for Mayor. It was the second election of City Council that I really let define me at the time. I honestly did not know how mean people could be.

I felt overwhelmed. I put my face out there on 4 x 8 foot signs and gave my heart and soul to a community I loved community service only to have my core values broken, rejected and unwanted. I was devastated to the extent that I was suicidal. When I look back now, I can't believe I allowed myself to care so much about what others thought. The City Council run came at a time when we were in a recession, and there was still a lot of uncertainty with the whole country. People wanted change. What it came down to is that they were afraid of change. And that fear guided their opinions. Anyone that "knew too much" was out, while anyone who was new at this was favorable. I fell into the category of knowing too much. I wasn't an incumbent like the other two candidates who didn't make it, but I had been attending meetings for two years, and I was ready to hit the ground running. I had served on every committee in town as chair, board member, president or associate. I knew I could make a difference. I wanted to BE the difference! I knew there was something bigger for me.

I had been challenged by a whole new group of bullies.
The biggest realization was that money and power did not motivate me and in politics, that is what it's all about.
I found that people would rather believe the gossip than verify the truth. That was hard to swallow. I had nothing to hide.

After the election was over, I was told that people were saying I didn't support the Utah Summer Games, which is an Olympic qualifier event. Nothing but gossip! I was the *Chair* of the Utah Summer Games Board of Commissioners, and my Real Estate company was a sponsor!

I was not one to back down from a challenge, and many knew that. They did not like it. They wanted a puppet who would just comply and say yes or look the other way. What I learned was that my heart definitely could not take serving in any of these positions, that of councillor or mayor. I did not and could not take the heartache it would have cost me to make decisions for 'the better good', while jeopardizing my integrity. Remember how I mentioned I cried every day as a child? It was almost an instant replay as an adult! I'd like to point out that I am known as a tough cookie, and it takes a lot to really make me cry. I thought I had tough skin until I lived through these experiences.

I swore after the second candidacy I would never do that to myself again.

Well… run for city council that is. So two years later apparently I got over it, and decided to run for Mayor!

This one wasn't such a disappointing loss. I was actually grateful I ran.

During that Mayoral run, my phone was tapped, and my computer was hacked. Post election, I was grateful and relieved to have my privacy back. This experience also allowed me to weed out more "so-called" friends. Through this, I noticed that this small town in Utah was predominantly patriarchal and that strong women were not favored. It was a shame, because so many women would have liked to contribute to their community. Instead, these women backed off or just moved away.

The morning after the election, I felt like such a loser. Rejected and dejected, lost as to what to do next… So as I was sulking, this song by Jonny Nash came to me. I started belting it out.

"I can see clearly now"

I can see clearly now the rain is gone.
I can see all the obstacles in my way
Gone are the dark clouds that got me blind
It's going to be a bright, bright sunshiny day

PEEKING BEHIND THE SCENES

I was happy to have been gifted another song to inspire and illuminate me in that moment. It had taken me three times running for a political office to realize this was not my journey!

After what I thought was the most horrific time in my life I realized nope, just another learning lesson. I went on to realize I was meant for more than who I was being.

What was next for me in the grand scheme of my life? What greatness was I to share with the world? How would I figure this out?
I wish I was the person then I have become now, but I had to experience the journey in order to get to where I am.

So what now? How could I make the impact that I wanted? Who was my tribe? Who did I really want to be serving? How could I be set for life? What did that even mean?
Only questions.

I didn't need to change what I was doing. I just needed to change who I was doing it for. My genius and my service were being wasted on the wrong people!
I realized I needed to find those who were like-minded and wanted to move forward in their life.

I love being an entrepreneur, thinking for myself and making my own decisions. My opinion and choices matter even if only to me, and I am happy I have created a life I love to wake up to every day. I influence and change the lives of others who want to move forward, who welcome change, and will stop at nothing until they get to the result. The biggest change I have been gifting people with is their mindset. Whatever they desire I am confident I can help them achieve it. I coach clients using tools including Hypnosis, specifically for people with PTSD. People who have had a lot of adversity and want to overcome their limiting beliefs and "clear the clutter" holding them back are part of my specialties. My favorite thing is when I witness breakthroughs happen in less than two hours. It's life changing for both my client and myself. It happens all of the time and the high I get from it rocks my world!

I have not figured my path all out yet, and I know at the same time that I am closer than I was yesterday, and tomorrow I will be closer than I am today.

We are all unique beings, and we don't have to prove anything to anyone. Practice what makes you happy, and then you will become what makes you happy. Life is short my friends. Be grateful for your challenges and hardships and remember they are all just lessons.

PEEKING BEHIND THE SCENES

Don't let anyone steal your sparkle. You have a purpose and if you don't know what it is yet, start digging. Find out what it is. There are many people who will come across your path in life that will bring out the best and the worst in you. I am happy to assist you in your journey. Search for good, search for wisdom, and then you will find the path that is right for you.

My Mantra:

Everyday is a new day to start over. Everyday is a new day to become better. Everyday is a new day to live my dreams.
~Holly Porter

I AM ENOUGH!

Theresia Valoczy

Theresia Valoczy is a #1 Bestselling Author, a Hypnotherapist, Archangel Life Coach and is Certified in Indigo Studies. Theresia coaches young people and women to help them discover their passion and for them to develop their individuality. Theresia's main aim is to teach people how to use their creative energy and the Universal Laws, as well as Angel Guidance to enhance their life.

www.spiritualparenting.eu

Chapter 13

Roots and Wings

By Theresia Valoczy

"If you know what you want, do not stand in the way of progress. Swim in the flow of opportunities, until you have reached your destination." Theresia Valoczy

Even as a child I knew I wanted to be a writer. I loved words. I loved the way they magically formed into a sentence and caused people's lives to change.

I used to focus all my energy on this purpose.

I did not come from a wealthy family. In Hungary, many people think that success is defined by the financial background of the man. I could never identify with this.

My parents could not offer me any financial backing, which would have helped my writing career enormously. They made up for it, however, by providing me with lots of emotional and spiritual support. They always said: "if this is your dream, just do it!"

Which I did.

I started with poems and essays that would delight my soul.

Now, I am a #1 International Best Selling Author. I created a best-selling book series, and I am the owner of a best-selling magazine publication. I am very grateful to the Universe for all the events that happened in my life. All of these events, whether good or bad, whether I liked them or not, contributed to who I am and where I am now.

In Hungary, I released two books. One was a private expenditure, meaning I self-published my book. I do not call it a success, but this was the first step towards realizing my own identity towards myself. I used a pen name for this first publication. Not only was I scared of the possible criticism this book would receive, but it played on my own internal fears too. I used my maiden name for the second book I published. The topic was on matriarchal culture and women issues. I was finally following the path of my soul and was revealing through my writings, who I really was.

Then I hit a low point in my life. Emotionally and mentally, I got into an unstable position. I had a dark cage close around me, which my husband had locked and kept the key.

There was no reason to complain. I had everything. The problem was that I was afraid of my husband's opinion of what I was up to. Seeing as he was a blue-collar worker, I was concerned that he would not approve of my writing career and perhaps even hinder me from doing so. Yet, I dared to write.

Since writing was not generating a proper source of income, I felt worthless.
And from this world full of worthless thoughts, my first spiritual novel was born. I worked on it when I could and when I heard the sound of my husband's car, I locked the documents up and concealed what I had written.

Then one day, an unexpected change occurred: my husband was diagnosed with severe heart disease. They put in an ICD device in his chest. It kept him alive, yet he required constant supervision. This lasted for an entire six months. He had always been the main breadwinner. Now he couldn't work anymore. Revenue from one day to the next was slowly but surely diminishing as the days progressed, which was also marked by a dramatic drop in lifestyle. Finally, the power service in our house was turned off.
This is what I now call my "hero era".

Some said we were back to living like in the prehistoric times, but I insisted that this period of my life was the most wonderful era that was revealed to me and that I had the privilege to live through. Life was perfectly simplified. There was no TV and no computer. It gave freedom to my soul.

Breakfast meditations in Nature, fresh herbs, the animals surrounding us, cozy cooking outdoors, candle light dinners and candle light baths. My creativity sprouted and eventually exploded.

Sometimes we have to lose what we think we call our stability in order to understand that it is our attitude that dictates the preservation of a good mental balance, and that it has nothing to do with money or any financial background in the first place.

I felt an old spark in me being revived. After a year and a half of nursing my husband, I felt that call again. The call for writing. The call for putting pen to paper. The pen and the paper is all the equipment needed by the writer. It doesn't need to be complicated. You can use the simplest of tools to create amazing artwork.

In the morning, I sat in my little garden and wrote. It was wonderful.

When we regained financial stability, our power service was restored, and my life resumed back to what it was. Yet I had developed a plan based on my angelic gifts. Out of my meditations was born the Teraxlation method, which is a relaxation technique for creating well-being.

PEEKING BEHIND THE SCENES

At the same time, I felt a calling to continue to learn English. I trusted my Angels with their guidance, and this led me to a Dr Joe Vitale and Dr Steve G.Jones course on the Law of Attraction. I continued with Hypnosis, Communication, Hypnotherapy, Past Life Regression, and Numerology.

Hungarian is my mother tongue. I was learning English by reading the material out loud and by watching the training videos. I took countless notes, looking for associations between the words, the sentence structure, and the harmonious connections.

I watched English language films, and a new goal was being formulated in my mind: I wanted to become an international best-selling author, and I wanted to do it by writing in English!

When I would say it out loud, people would laugh. One person even said: "My Girl, you are Hungarian. Keep your feet on the ground!" I could have taken it badly, but instead, I saw it as them giving me a gentle reminder that I had roots and not wings. I immediately thought to myself: why not both? Why could I not have roots and wings at the same time? The goal was huge in my soul. I heard that calling with my heart pounding. The synchronicities in my life have shown me that I am walking the right course. I can certainly not let English not being my native language, stop me.

A friend of mine soon answered my prayers. She asked me to write in her upcoming book: *Manifesting a New Life*. My heart was throbbing. I was overjoyed. But then the ego started to list all of the possible problems: I was no good, I did not have enough knowledge in the English language, and who was I kidding?

One little devil after another popped up.
Nevertheless, I made a list of what this opportunity could bring me. I chose to illustrate this list in pictures and created a photo album of it.

One day, I went on a picnic with my friend. I took out the photo album and showed it to him. He leafed through it, smiled, and then moved in closer to me. He opened the album again and pointing to the first picture he asked me to tell him how it felt to me to become an international best-selling author.

It was then that I realized that once I knew and recognized my Divine Purpose's call, and I did not resist against it or look for excuses, everything was going to work out just fine and unfold quite naturally. My friend showed me, I could do it.

That day, my ego defeated reasoning.

PEEKING BEHIND THE SCENES

My dreams came true. The book became a bestseller, and I became an international best-selling author. I was so pleased with myself and was glad I had written and submitted my chapter. I began to appreciate myself, and I felt true happiness.

Then came the birth of my own Conscious Creator series: an anthology followed by magazines. Did I experience difficulties with having very few relationships around the world and my language difficulties? I certainly did. But I pushed through and stayed committed to my dream. The anthology book became a bestseller upon its release and even number one on the Canadian bestseller list. And every magazine edition that has been published has made it on the Amazon Top 100.

There have been and still are daily hindering factors. I have roots that show where I come from. I want to keep them intact, as they are part of me. And I have wings, which allow me to fly way up in the sky. I trust myself in the ability of both my roots and my wings. The Universe is perfect in transporting me to where I want to go. My only job is to keep my faith and my belief alive.

I use my Teraxlation method to realize my dreams and accept my current conditions. When I am facing difficulties, I take a deep breath through my crown chakra and breathe out through my roots. I put my hands on my heart and say: thank you for allowing me to be a successful writer.

What I went through was not easy, but it is now behind me.

Many times I could have given up, but I chose not to.
My calling and my purpose are so strong that I could not turn my back on them now.

Having lived through this process myself, my advice on this is that when you feel the fire in your soul, if you feel like you must stretch out your wings, do not hold back.

Your past circumstances do not define you. They do not describe your success. You define you! You are the creator of your success. You have achieved success because you exist. Allow your soul to journey back to you. Allow yourself to soar and become who you were born to be.

Find your passion and develop it. Nourish yourself every day with love. Nurse your passion, take care of it every day and make sure it never gets damaged. Care for it like a mother does her child. Embrace it, love it, carry on a conversation with it. Get to know it better. Create that bond between you and your passion.

Close your eyes and imagine your dream has been realized, that it has come true. Feel it, hear it, see yourself in the role that you want to be in. Give thanks to the amazing realization. Be happy, and enjoy the moment. Ask from your dream what do you need and what can I give to it. How can I reach my dreams? Wait for the answer. Wait to hear the sound of the intuitive channel, the feeling within, then open your eyes and be filled with this magical energy. Now put the necessary steps in play to recreate this emotion and this scenario.

True success comes from having deep insights concerning our life. It's about learning our necessary lessons, which are unique to each of us, and to awaken ourselves from them.
Each event shows us the way while acting as a mirror. If you took a look and did not like it, change it from the inside, for this self-awareness and spiritual development are necessary in order to grow. This causes us to wake up. From the outside, it seems only like the result. However, this is just an illusion. This is the surface of the lake water. What lies beneath it, what lurks in the background, whether it is good or bad, are blessings. My blessings have personally led me to where I am now. I would not have wanted it any other way.

I admit I have a language difficulty, and I often get looked at strangely. Sometimes I still feel fear when I stand ready to take my next step. Yet excitement fills me when I need to speak English, and I am able to block out that fear. Does it matter that I have obstacles in front of me all the time like this? Yes! It matters. Each problem I have to solve on my path will bring me more experience in life. I think it is a matter of perspective to see these problems as gifts we receive while

striving on other things in the meantime, regardless of what is around us.
The important thing is to discover the brilliance in ourselves.

The brilliance of the soul is real, and so is the divine purpose of my calling that is leading my life, showing me the way.

PEEKING BEHIND THE SCENES

Compiled by **JENNIFER LOW**

Agnes Kazmierczak

Agnes Kazmierczak is an internationally recognized ballroom dance champion, winning many titles including being placed among the top 12 couples in the world and performed Live to Michael Bublee on Dancing With The Stars.

Agnes believes that dance reveals one's soul and is the ultimate way of expression. She is a renowned coach, examiner, and adjudicator for the famous dance franchise, Arthur Murray International, which has been teaching people how to dance for over 100 years. In 2016, following her passion for gemstones and design, Agnes launched her jewelry brand *Jioya*.

www.agneskazmierczak.com
www.jioya.com

Chapter 14

Dance to the Music of Your Heart

By Agnes Kazmierczak

When I was 7 years old and went to my first ballroom dancing class, it never crossed my mind that I would eventually be writing a chapter in a book about it and much less, be an inspiration to others for it. I never thought that I would eventually, in the future, win several championship titles, compete and perform all over the world, teach, judge and have an opportunity to perform live on TV in front of 20 million people. Least of all, I never thought that my childhood passion would offer me a life of fulfillment, growth and joy, through a career that not only allowed the expression of my soul, but also having a positive impact on the lives of others.

I often get asked what my biggest success and accomplishment is. I have a hard time answering, but how about this: I got invited to share my story because someone thought that my experiences and lessons could help others. And if my story can inspire someone to follow their heart, and believe that with faith and determination, dreams can come true, then there it is, my biggest accomplishment.

Compiled by **JENNIFER LOW**

Let me tell you my story:

It was one of those cold and dark winter days. I heard my mom's voice saying it was time to wake up. I had that feeling in my stomach again. I didn't want to get up. It was 5 in the morning, I was still tired from my previous evening's dance practice and it was dark and so cold outside of my bed. By 6am we were out the door taking a bus, a train and having to walk the last part of the two-hour commute. We would arrive at school by 8am, just in time to change into my ballet clothes, make my hair, warm up and start the ballet class. I was attending this National Ballet School where thousands of kids would take exams every year for the 24 available spots. It was a privilege to be there and we were reminded of it every day.

The first two hours were always the toughest. We had a Russian teacher. Her name was Alla Karpuchinova. I will never forget her face and her charcoal black hair. She was tiny yet so powerful and frightening. The moment she took her first step into the room, everybody went quiet and practice began. And I would feel the knot in my stomach again. I don't remember her ever smiling or ever saying any positive words. She would dig her nails into our legs until they bled and sat on us while we stretched so we couldn't give up. Facing the pain, we kept going.

I remember we had a lady playing piano for us in the morning during our ballet class. I would get lost in the beautiful music

PEEKING BEHIND THE SCENES

in order to not feel the pain.

Today, when I go for my hot yoga class to stay in shape, the feeling of pushing myself to stretch is one of the most enjoyable and rewarding sensations I get to experience.

For me, it's like a metaphor for life because to grow and expand, one needs to go past one's comfort zone.

Every day around 3, my mom would be there to pick me up and take me to my grandma's, who lived half way between my school and home. We would eat dinner together, do some homework and go to my evening ballroom dance class. Every evening was like a competition. All the parents would watch while the kids danced. I liked to perform, and I always felt like I was being scored by the judges: what I wore, how I moved, how much I rested, and how quickly I picked up new moves. My teacher was brilliant, yet he treated us like adults. There was very little play time and lots of constant striving to become better. By 10 o'clock in the evening, we were home. I remember the blissful feeling of lying in bed and closing my eyes to sleep, knowing that in a few hours the same process would begin again.

I also remember different kinds of mornings. Waking up to the smell of self-tan on my skin, the pinching of the curling rolls in my hair, the innocent feeling of incredible excitement and great anticipation, accompanied by the butterflies in my stomach and just the feeling of happiness. Those were the mornings of my ballroom dance competitions. It was a magical world, and I absolutely loved it. I was obsessed with it. And by the age of 14, my dream came true. My partner and I became National Polish Champions in the Junior Division.

At the age of 16, I got an incredible offer to become the partner of a very talented dancer from Sweden. It was an amazing opportunity, and I was ecstatic. But it came with a price: I had to move to Sweden. I didn't know the language: nor Swedish nor English. I also had to leave my friends and family behind and start a new chapter in a country I didn't know anyone.
It's kind of crazy when I think back, but my love for dance was stronger than anything.

Years later, my mom told me how hard it was for her, letting me go. She cried many nights, worrying about me. Looking back, I could only imagine what she was going through. And I am endlessly grateful that despite everything, she still made it possible. She had to take on three jobs to support my dancing and living in Sweden, and it was a constant struggle, as income in Poland was significantly lower than most other countries in Europe.

I spent almost 3 years in Sweden. It was incredibly challenging and difficult. Despite the fact that my partner's parents treated me like a daughter, and did everything to make me feel like I was at home, I often felt lonely and that I somehow did not fit in. I also missed my family a lot.

Dance wise, we had a lot of success. We became National Champions several times and represented Sweden at the World and European Championships.

Towards the end of my time there, my dance partner started to lose focus. He wasn't as committed and didn't want to practice. We were teenagers, and he seemed to be more interested in hanging out with friends or going to parties rather than practicing. I was getting more and more frustrated as I had given up so much to dance with him.

Then came an opportunity to dance with another phenomenal dancer from Italy and I couldn't resist. I needed to go there to try out and see if it was a good fit. Since my family could not afford a plane ticket, it took me 27 hours on a bus to get there. He was very well known and one of the top dancers at the time. I was thrilled when he decided to partner up with me.

Once again, I had to move to another country, but this time I had a lot more experience and courage. I moved into a small room by the studio and would literally practice day and night. In one month, we had made it into the top 12 couples at the most prestigious ballroom dance competition in the world. I couldn't believe that this was really happening. All these glorious achievements and yet, at the same time, I was miserable.

I hated everything about my life in Italy and the partnership too. As brilliant of a dancer as he was, quite honestly, he was a horrible person. He was mean, unreasonable, and abusive. I later learned that he had physically hurt his previous partner to the point where she ended up in the hospital. I knew I could have an incredible career with him, but at the same time, I was dreading every practice and started to hate dancing.

Finally one day, I had enough and decided to go back to Poland. I was heartbroken and didn't know what to do with myself. I finished high school but had no interest in going to college and studying just anything for the sake of it. I didn't know what I wanted, and I was lost.

A few months passed, and by digging deep into my soul, I found I was itching. Although I was happy to be with my family again, I was so hungry for a new challenge and a new adventure. The more time went by, the more I knew I did not want to stay in Poland. One recurring question kept coming up: "how could I make my childhood dream of moving to the United States come true?" I really wanted to move to the US. I had always had this deep feeling that it would be a place for me.

PEEKING BEHIND THE SCENES

I took action! I started to look for connections in the US and I got in touch with some dance friends from my old studio, who had moved to California years before. I was thrilled to find out that the studio there was looking for a teacher and that they were interested in bringing me over.

The first thing I noticed when I landed in LA was the palm trees. I remember thinking how exotic they looked to me and I loved it.

My first year was pretty tough. I started to teach full time right away. Although I was happy teaching, I noticed that it did not fulfill me entirely. I started looking for a dance partner. He was very hard to find. My prayers were answered when after several unsuccessful tryouts, I got an email from a very good dancer in Germany. I didn't want to move again and I was relieved when he decided that he would gladly relocate to LA to dance with me.

It was my longest, most successful and most enjoyable partnership in my career. We both had the same mindset and even though we wanted to be as good as we possibly could, it was also very important to respect each other and enjoy the journey.

We very quickly became one of the top couples in the US and had a lot of international success as well. There were a lot of ups and downs, accompanied by tears of joy and tears of defeat. But I could not have asked for a better partner and I thank him for all the memories from the bottom of my heart.

What I am especially proud of is that we were known for having a very original style. I think it's because we always tried to dance to the music of our hearts.

Dancing, just like life, can be very subjective and there is definitely more than one way to live. You can either follow your heart and be true to yourself, or suppress that and try to fit in and please others. As much as you can learn and take advice from other people, it is your life, your dance, your song to sing.
So don't give away that gift. It's the only thing you will ever own!

With this philosophy in mind, this year I took my own advice and jumped in to a passionate project of mine. After months of intense work, my jewelry brand *Jioya* came to life. It combines my passion for nature, beauty, art and metaphysical energies in a way that could help everyone attract and manifest one's deepest desires through the healing powers of gemstones. I believe that every woman just like every diamond is one of a kind and eternally beautiful. Just like the depth of a gemstone it's the depth of our soul which makes us captivating and unique. And I believe that true beauty is the beauty from within. Just like the gemstones come from the inside of the Earth, our physical beauty comes from the inside of our souls. My jewelry pieces are a manifestation and a reminder of that.

As I was writing my story for this book, I got into a car accident. I was blessed to walk away from it in one piece. Yet it made me reflect on life. I think about all those people who don't get to be so lucky. It made me think: "what if I would never have been able to dance or walk ever again?" In those moments, the perspective of life changes, and it makes us realize that we don't have time, the way we usually think about it. That at any given moment, everything could change.

Today when I go for my long walks on the beach in Santa Monica and look to the ocean, sometimes I can't believe that all of it is real... I think back to where I came from and the contrast between my past and my present. I often wonder if it was destiny or whether I made it happen? I think it will always be a mystery to me, but one thing I know for sure is that regardless all of the pain, the difficulties, and the challenges, 1 always quietly believe that I have the right to fight for my dreams, and that they can come true.

We don't always know what we want or what our life mission should be, but I believe that our greatest task in life is to find out what it is. And if I can leave you with one final thought: don't just follow blindly and operate your life on autopilot. Do some soul searching, do the work to realize what lights you up, what makes you come alive, and start dancing to the music of your heart!

"The two most important days in your life are the day you are born, and the day you find out why." -Mark Twain

PEEKING BEHIND THE SCENES

Roberta Weber Calabró

Roberta Weber Calabró is a PR based in London, founder of "Steps to Fly Company" and author of "The Complete Guide Steps to Fly in London". She writes for the Blog "Viajando Bem e Barato", for the "BN- Notícias em Português" newspaper and has a program on RBG radio. In 2015, she created "Community Migreat for Brazilians in UK".

Passionate about words and travels, she left Brazil in 2010 to live and experience new beginnings, difficulties, and victories abroad (Italy, Spain, and England). In doing so, she found out her true mission: helping people realize their dreams to live abroad.

Email: roberta@stepstofly.com
Facebook: www.facebook.com/stepstofly/
Linkedin https://uk.linkedin.com/in/roberta-weber- calabró-558ba539

Chapter 15

Steps to Fly
7 Steps to Transforming your Dream of Living Abroad Into a Challenging and Enchanting Reality

By Roberta Weber Calabró

Some might say success is to feel satisfaction after accomplishing something or making lots of money. Others would say it is having time for their children. For me, however, success is the realisation of a strong pre-defined goal, one that often needs to be discovered within and achieved somehow. The big secret is to discover and see it clearly as a path made of small and big steps. I will tell you *when* I discovered my purpose and *how* I started to apply this belief into my life in order to make my dreams (and other people's dreams) come true. In my case, my dream was to live abroad and have a life experience away from my country.

Presentation

"A destination is never a place, but a new way of seeing things", said Henry Miller. Nowadays, living abroad is the dream of many people for a number of reasons: escaping routine, financial insecurity, frustration at work, love disillusion, longing for adventure, or improving some aspects of life. However, many give up half way through. After having the first spark of your inner motivation comes the question: what are the steps to take once I have decided to live abroad and how do I get ready for the new life?

My experience

I was born in the South of Brazil and have always been passionate about communication and human relations. Throughout my childhood, my parents taught me to love traveling, so I went on school trips, lived in different cities, and at age 11, I flew for the first time to Rio de Janeiro. While in College, curious to discover the different cultures of my own country, I crossed Brazil by bus, which took me almost 5 days. I have always sought University scholarships abroad, but I never got one. Living abroad was such a big dream for me, as I understood it as a necessary challenge to grow, mature, learn languages, explore new places, and get to know different people and cultures, as well as myself. How was I to accomplish this among my fears of leaving my comfort zone, my internal indecisions, and the lack of money? And that's only a few of the challenges. I did not know where to start and although there were many paths in front of me I was not able to see any of them.

PEEKING BEHIND THE SCENES

My preparation

I graduated in Public Relations in 2009. At that time I had a boyfriend and a stable job. On my graduation day, while I was picking up my diploma, a song was playing. It spoke of butterflies. On that festive evening, surrounded by the people I loved the most, I realised how strong my desire was, to fly in search of my dreams. I understood that a dream is only a vision without action, and doing something is necessary to move forward. Yes, that was the beginning of a new time.

Because I had Italian grandparents, I was entitled to apply for an Italian citizenship, so I could legally live and work in Europe. Hiring an agent to go through the process was really expensive, and I did not have the required amount of money. Carrying out the process on my own would reduce the cost. I researched which documents were necessary, and I started working extra hours to save money. I read books, researched and heard stories of people who left everything behind to start fresh abroad. That strengthened me emotionally. I also studied Italian and bought Euros not even knowing if I would end up using them. I enjoyed every single step for it made me feel closer to realisation. My best friend Flor, who was living in Spain at that time, encouraged me. Being surrounded by helpful people was paramount in believing I could make it happen. One morning, sitting at my aunt Milena's kitchen table, I realised I was on the right track.

The decisive moment

Everyone has experienced situations in which they had to decide which way to go while being aware of the existence of two paths, each leading in a different direction, and which have the power to change the course of one's life. That is why I consider that morning the true "bridge" between my plan and my action that led me to successfully reach my goal. My aunt Milena asked me if I was sure I wanted to live abroad. With conviction, I replied YES and on the same day, she contacted a friend in Genoa asking if he would kindly help me with my stay in Italy during my citizenship process. Alfredo, whom I consider an angel, replied **yes** immediately, and that trigged feelings of joy and excitement mixed with fear and anxiety for the months leading up to my departure.

First steps abroad

Bags packed and crying goodbyes, there I was, sitting on the plane, knowing that there would be no return. Was that the correct decision? My Italian was not good, and I was alone! When will I see my family again? Even though I was so well prepared, leaving home brought up doubts. I just closed my eyes and embarked on my enchanting and challenging adventure.

PEEKING BEHIND THE SCENES

Alfredo welcomed me at the airport in Milan. He and his family were very kind, and in my first month, they spoiled me with the best breads, cheeses, olive oil, and wines at their summer home in Tuscany. In my second month, we were back in Genoa. He took me to school, helped me with all my documents, received me in his house and when the winter arrived, I moved in with his 94-year-old mother, Anna, in her house by the sea. She had a difficult personality, but taught me a lot and told me stories about World War II. This situation reminded me of my own grandparents, who left Genoa's port in 1940, with their four small children to head to South Brazil in search of a better life.

Despite those special moments, leaving my comfort zone also brought me sadness and melancholy, longing and loneliness. I remember calling my mother one snowy day, telling her that I was planning to go back home, but I had to carry on and follow my dream. Those were months of learning. To make a bit of money, I worked as a gardener, a cook and as a silver cleaner in Anna's house. Finally, two days before the Christmas of 2010, my Italian papers arrived. With plans in place to move to Madrid, I thanked everyone and said goodbye. In Spain, Flor and her housemate Alberto, were my new guardian angels.

The challenges in Madrid

Spain was in a huge economic crisis at the time. I had fears of not finding work. I did not speak the language and had very little money. Where was I starting, what were the paths? But I was optimistic and persistently left my CV in different places, always in search of opportunity. My turning point came a month later. I was selected for an interview with the giant ice cream company Haagen Dazs. Unable to speak Spanish, I asked the director for a chance to prove how capable I was, even after being told that I would not last a week of cleaning toilets and preparing ice cream. Two days later, I was in my uniform, and six months later I was promoted as the store supervisor leading fourteen employees.

While in Spain, I met amazing people, made friends for life, and travelled to wonderful places. I was even able to make my mother's dream come true: to travel to Europe for the first time in her life. I worked hard too, but suddenly I felt that it was time to move again. Flor and I decided to head to England. It took us five months to plan everything. Debora, an old friend from College, who was already in London, helped us finding a room in the western part of the city. After two years in Spain, we were saying goodbye and starting again.

PEEKING BEHIND THE SCENES

New life in London

On a cold morning of 2013, I was crossing the beautiful Tower Bridge. I was tired and had many expectations and doubts. Did I make the right decision? How will I work without speaking English? Do I have enough money to survive in an expensive city? Then I thought: what if I repeat those steps that worked for me before and cut out those that did not?

During the initial months, we shared a beautiful apartment with five other girls. Again, the Universe, combined with my own efforts, showed me *The Cortisso Accommodation* - the renting company and owner of the flat we lived in. Twenty days later I asked the director, Leandro Marcondes, for an opportunity and succeeded. Soon I was hanging out with people from various countries and cultures. They all had enthusiasm and fears, hopes and dreams. Some were well prepared, and others very lost and in need of guidance. I began to see myself in each of them and felt almost responsible for their well-being. Perhaps there was a way to repay all the help I had received.

On July 23rd that same year, a life-changing opportunity came my way. Leandro offered me a last-minute invitation to attend the course "Mission to Millions", in Warsaw. His two friends had their visas denied just one day before their departure, so I was going to Poland. This four day course was intended to help you discover your purpose in life, through reflecting on your own history and vision of your future. Those were magical and intense days. I was there with people from all over the world just feeling that everything around me was moving in tune with the Universe. I thought I had in my hands, the opportunity to make a difference in people's lives through my own experience. I thought to myself that if I had been able to start over in three different countries and be successful in all my objectives, I could help people who have the same dream as me. I could help them set up their life in a country that would be new for them.

Steps to Fly

I returned to London determined to make my mission a reality. I gathered texts, thoughts, and memories of my journey so far and sought answers. What had helped me achieve my goals and overcome my own challenges while living abroad? Why was it that some people manage to move abroad and others do not? What makes someone who lives abroad a winner?

Here is my answer: most who have managed to achieve their goals have done this, because of two main factors: 1- They prepared themselves better 2- They had a strong pre-defined objective.
With this in mind, they persisted every day.

PEEKING BEHIND THE SCENES

Living abroad is a process like any other, made of small and big steps. It begins by discovering what your end goal is.

That is why I started my company *Steps to Fly* – I inspire and prepare people to live abroad. And then I created a _7 Steps to Fly System_ to prepare and show people how to do that.

PLAN

1 - DISCOVERY
The discovery of your goal and focusing on it are indispensable when starting this journey.

2 - RESEARCH AND PLANNING
Whatever your plans are, you need to research all the necessary information about the new city and country and schedule everything you want to do beforehand.

3 - EMOTIONS
As excitement can blur emotions, psychological preparation and seeking support is crucial to face and cope with challenges.

ACTION

4 - REAL PREPARATION AND CHOICES

After the planning phase, it is time to take action and to consider looking at finances, booking accommodations, courses, flights, and connect with this new place.

5 - TRANSITION AND CHECKLIST

There is no turning back! It's time to enjoy the last month and review everything. It's time to fly.

6- SURPRISE AND OVERCOMING CHALLENGES
The first three months are full of surprises, made up of positive and negative experiences. You just need to adapt and overcome challenges to be successful. It's part of the travelled road.

7 - SUCCESS

Success of your goal depends on how you are able to take advantage of every opportunity, knowing that each step is part of your future success – as long as you set your mind to it. If you have to change the way to achieve it, just do so.

PEEKING BEHIND THE SCENES

note: I realised that having access to information on the targeted city is crucial for the first steps. This is why in 2015 I launched the *Steps to Fly in London Guide* in Portuguese, a 460-page digital guide with all the necessary information for those who want to live here. In 2016, I created a small version (*A simple Guide for life and success in the city of London*) in other languages.

Helping people around the world

Steps to Fly and I have already helped more than 500 people who have come to live abroad. The most recent example is that of Fernando Piotto Leonardi, 34. In January 2015 he told me his dream was to become a pizzaiolo in Italy. We went through every step of the process and in July 2016, I received photos of the conclusion of his course in Florence.

In February 2016, *Steps to Fly* won its own daily show (Passos para Voar) on Radio RBG, the first online Brazilian radio in the world.

Success

My experience both in Brazil and abroad has involved mistakes and accomplishments, failures and successes. In the end, my greatest lesson was that I have discovered my objectives, planned my path and prepared myself carefully. I flew, I was surprised, I excelled, and I built from the ground up. It is important to celebrate even the smallest victory every day.

What I consider success today is much different from how I understood it before. Knowing that someone is reading my guide, because it saves them money and time, is rewarding, and their successes are reflected upon my own. I felt successful when I recently received a hug from a newly arrived couple and was told that our conversation, a year ago, was crucial in making their dream of living abroad come true. The same happens when I hear of people saying how assured and confident they felt during their trip preparation once they had gotten in contact with us.

Do I feel successful every day? Of course not, we are made of all these positive and negative feelings. However, I feel successful, because I am able to help people achieve their own goals. It truly fulfills my purpose. And let's never forget: a strong pre-defined goal is the key to beginning this new path in your life.

PEEKING BEHIND THE SCENES

Lison Ouellette

Lison Ouellette is a unique French Canadian furniture and interior designer. Beginning her career in 1986, Lison quickly became a top in her field. Over the past 25 years, her passion has continued to fuel her creativity. She has become a recognized expert in her field.

Whether designing for residential homes or commercial spaces, Lison believes that her designs should be reflective of the individual's lifestyle or organization. She works closely with her clients, assessing their needs, style and space to create personalized designs that are functional and stunning. Lison takes care to ensure that all of her designs are unique creations.

www.lisonartfurniture.com
www.facebook.com/lison.af
1.604.657.8184

Chapter 16

Stick To Your Passion

By Lison Ouellette

Prior to participating in this book, I found myself doing an exercise on success. I was to analyze each of my big markers in life and in business and decide if they would qualify as a success or as a failure.

Many people see me as a success. I carry qualities of confidence and competency. I am a visionary with a competitive edge. I know my craft! And best of all, I love what I do!

I do consider myself a success as well, although most likely in a very different light than others see it, because it is my story and I have lived it. Some see the Lison of the present moment, the one that you see right here, right now. I see the Lison who has conquered any and every challenge that has come to pass. Some have even said to me I am very lucky. That's when I stop and think to myself that most don't know I have fought countless battles to live my passion and have worked every minute of my life for this "luck".

Compiled by **JENNIFER LOW**

I learned my craft very early on in life, because of the influencers I had around me. My grandfather was a millworker. While in his workshop, I would build doll beds by his side. My great aunt, who was a seamstress, taught me how to sew. With whatever material she could spare, I would make bedding for my wooden doll beds. And so started my journey to my current design career. My great aunt was my true guide. She taught me to always live my passion first and foremost. I thought her wise and made sure to follow her advice.

My success streak started at the end of the 1980s. Fresh out of school, I had applied for a job at a design firm that had its own millwork, and paint and upholstery shop. I was excited and enthusiastic to meet the owner and show off my portfolio to him, but he simply said: "I heard about you. You are hired!"
Nine months later I was to become their top designer. I was even managing projects from the millwork shop division, as well as selling furniture to some of the big stores. This job was to be my real life learning experience in this business.
This success helped reinforce my confidence in myself.

One time, I found myself by the liquor store's head office so I walked in. Shortly after, I walked out with 4-5 rolls of plans to quote on. I had jumped on the opportunity and yes, I had won contracts from a major company that my boss had been challenged with, and had tried to obtain for years.

PEEKING BEHIND THE SCENES

In 1991, I branched off on my own. I opened up a design studio in an office I shared with an architect. Success found me very quickly. I landed many contracts in the two main shopping malls in my town. I was also growing my design business in parallel with that of my then-husband. As a contractor, he built some of my projects. We made a great and successful team back then.

One day, as I stood in my kitchen, I found myself looking around me and thinking: I have the big home, the beautiful yard with the swimming pool, three cars in the driveway, my dream job, and a multitude of other real estate assets. I realized at that moment that at twenty five years old, I had the material possessions of someone in their forties. I was living the successful life. Yet I was so busy working, I was never actually able to enjoy the fruit of my labour.

After personally bumping into some health issues, my husband and I decided to sell everything we owned and take a year to get away, to do something else, to disconnect. We left Quebec and disappeared to Costa Rica for a while. We ended up in Vancouver, Canada in February of 1996. It was while I stood on Prospect Point, admiring the breath taking scenery of the mountains meeting the sea, while viewing West Vancouver and North Vancouver, with torrential rains pouring down and raccoons circling around us, it was in that moment that I fell in love with that city and have been living there ever since.

Compiled by **JENNIFER LOW**

Here, as a follow up to what we had grown in Quebec, we started a company together, my husband and I: me as the designer, and he as the contractor. We worked it for about a year and again, success found us early on. The business grew at an exponential rate.

And then, …the first big life challenge happened.

It was May of 1998. Upon discovering that my husband was leading a double life, I gave him an ultimatum. He took the option to leave and walked out of my life. My only issue remained that I had not thought about the financial ramifications it would have on me. I kind of got caught with my pants down. Anything that fell under expenses was in my name. Meanwhile, anything that was qualified as "asset" was in his name. I had been with this man for twelve years and had placed immense trust in him, and here he was, leaving me in a pickle. From one day to the next I had lost my husband, my job, I had no assets to my name, and I did not even have a penny in the bank! I was fortunate that the rent for that month had already been covered, but I knew I had to come up with a plan, and quickly! Otherwise it meant that my 5 year old son and myself were going to end up on the streets.

It was time for me to reassess.
I didn't want to tell my family about this, because I knew how

201

easy it would have been to be lured back to them in Quebec. It would have been easy to go home and be taken care of and protected. I wanted my next step to be MY decision.

I asked myself what was it that I truly wanted?
The final answer was that I was in love with Vancouver. With my answer firmly in place, and barely any English, the next natural question then became: how do I go about this and what's my next logical step to proceed forward?

My plan was to start by finding a community I could communicate with and that could help me. So I went to the francophone center in Vancouver, specifically to check out the sector in business development. A lovely lady hooked me up and I obtained two projects from that one initial visit. That helped me get back on my feet a little. I still had to go on social assistance for six months, which I had vowed never to do. Desperate times call for desperate measures. I even had a friend of mine help me out by lending me money to cover the bare necessities.

By October of that year, I was incorporating my business *L.O. Interior Design and Management* and the projects kept on coming. That October was also the month that I sat down with a financial planner and made sure I was getting life insurance and anything else I needed to cover my kid and myself and to protect us from this ever happening again. I was ready to climb my new mountain.

Almost ten years later, I was faced with what seemed like an instant replay… I was in a serious relationship with a man for 6 years, when in September of 2007 I found out I was pregnant. The man I was with was very adamant about not wanting kids, so he left. My decision was clear: I was keeping the baby. And yes, I was to raise this one on my own too. The only difference was that this time I knew I didn't have a chance of seeing the streets. I had spent the last ten years carefully building my assets and being actively aware of and involved in my own financial management. Nope, what I lived with this baby was quite different.

In May of 2008 I gave birth to a beautiful baby boy. I was completely passionate about my baby and I was just as passionate about my work. So I blended the two of them together. I remembered my mother's words saying that a baby isn't supposed to stop you from living. In fact, a baby will usually allow you to push yourself further and grow. And that's exactly what happened, quite literally actually. My baby went everywhere with me. He created this wonderful energy around each project. He would provide almost as much joy for some of my clients as he did to my own life. And my business grew. I was getting projects that were much larger than what I was used to.

PEEKING BEHIND THE SCENES

In fact, in 2012, as we were just returning from Mexico, I signed three contracts in the same week. Unheard of until then in my personal performance track record. I was proud of myself!

Then I had two car accidents within three months of each other. After the second one, for the first time in my life, I was truly facing fear. Everything I had faced before were merely challenges. This time, I had to face real fear! This second accident caused me to put my "invincibility" into perspective. The biggest one of those fears evidently being: if something happened to me, what would happen to my children?

It is in what I call this "dark period" of mine that *Lison Art Furniture* was born. This was a dream business of mine, one that was completely driven by my passion to create and where clients would willingly seek me out. I jumped in with both feet without casting too much attention to some of the details. I had amazing credit so I approached the bank to front me some capital. Everything was set. We were getting ready to sign and then one thing after another happened to this bank manager who was in charge of my file. A birth, a death, a marriage, you name it, she had it. I figured it was a done deal as I had been approved and the only thing left to do was for the papers to be signed. I got myself a lease and I started my business. I could not wait any longer for her life to unfurl so I proceeded to move forward with mine.

Well! Wouldn't you know... By the time she was able to get back to me, the deal was not "valid" anymore as now I was onto the 'next stage' of my business. She clearly told me that now I had changed the circumstances. I was not borrowing from a business plan, I was to be granted the money by showing numbers. Seriously?!?! My jaw dropped. I had just opened my doors to a very capital-intensive business. Of course my numbers wouldn't look amazing! I had just started! Her last words were that when I had significant dynamic numbers, it would be a good time to approach them again.

Fine! I would figure this one out on my own again. And I did. I made it work, cuz I always do.

Two years later, I was approached by an investor. This would have meant fantastic exposure for me and my company, and the access to that money would have given me enormous leaway to produce creatively, but within very strict limitations. The proposed contract conditions were suggesting I become the working puppet. Selling my soul in exchange for the money did not make sense to me. I was working from a point of passion, and I knew working for someone else would not be viable, because it would simply turn off my life-light completely. I would have rather closed my doors than to relinquish the power to someone else this way. I gladly walked away from that opportunity.

PEEKING BEHIND THE SCENES

The next big hurdle I had to surmount with *Lison Art Furniture* had to do with the people I kept around me. I was moving forward with some challenges, but still fine with this business, when my accountant strongly advised me to close my doors. I was initially surprised about this. I started noticing how drained I became when I was around her. It was her negative energy beaming off of her that I was capturing. Then it dawned on me that this professional did not believe in me and did not have an open-minded way of thinking. If I wanted to be successful, I needed to keep people around me who welcomed growth, who believed in me and in my work, and who supported me at 100%. Needless to say, I fired her.

Lison Art Furniture is still growing and thriving at the moment. Even though I know my craft, I often feel like I have embarked on this big boat, I have already left the harbor, and I am learning how to navigate it, as it has drifted in a different direction than I was expecting. I am allowing myself to be guided by my vision and by my goal and I am perfecting my navigation skills, as I get further into deeper waters.

That said, I am so committed to my passion and to my success that I am currently working with a coach. Her role is to teach me how to navigate this boat in the most appropriate way that will fit me. She is showing me how to read the compass to my passion, and is making sure I stay on the right course. Her input and her accountability are priceless!

After four years in business with *Lison Art Furniture*, I have a ton of satisfied customers, who are floored by my work, and who actually keep coming back for more. I am grateful for all of my wonderful clients, as it is really a demonstration to me of their belief in me. I deliver their exclusively designed pieces to them, I design their home and even design their business. In return, they do not only bring me business success, but also personal success, which becomes my personal satisfaction.

As I continue to grow, I am currently still writing my life story.
What I tell myself is that in the end, we all leave this earth. So how do I measure my success if I have this attitude that we are all doomed? Put it this way: when I'm 80 or 90 years old, I want to be able to look back at my life and know that I am completely at peace with every decision I made, with everything I have lived, and with the legacy I leave behind. This peace from within will be my ultimate success!

PEEKING BEHIND THE SCENES

Aldona Konkol

Aldona was born and raised in a small town in Poland and came to Canada when she was 14. Her first job as a travel agent lasted 13 years. Even though she was successful and wore many hats in the company, life changed after having kids. Aldona knew she wanted more. After successfully flipping a few homes, a career as a Realtor became an obvious choice. Her passion lies in designing, staging and selling homes. Integrity and honesty govern Aldona's work and she continues to live out her passion and dream on the daily!

Email: aldonakondol@yahoo.ca

Direct number: 416-986-0893

Chapter 17

Follow Your Dreams
My Life, My Way!

By Aldona Konkol

I have always considered myself to be a very determined person. Perhaps that's how I was born. Perhaps my mother influenced me into becoming so. I was the eldest of four kids and I was made aware quite early on that I was going to be an example for all my siblings. My mother would remind me that if I was stupid, then they were all going to be stupid. I felt this responsibility weighing down on my young shoulders, so I watched what I did. Every step had its purpose.

I was born in Poland. Life was OK there. I was surrounded by friends and family. My dad was working in Canada and would send money over. We weren't rich, but we had a pretty good lifestyle because of his efforts.

Then, in one day, life changed for all of us!

There was a big accident at the construction site where my dad worked. My uncle died, and my father was very badly injured. Life changed pretty drastically from that moment on. My mother couldn't keep going back and forth to visit and take care of him anymore. My dad needed someone by his side. The choice was clear! Within six months we were packed and relocating to another country more than half a world away! I was fourteen at the time. I was going to attend high school without knowing a word of English! There were so many changes happening in a short amount of time, yet we had no choice but to learn to adapt.

Life was tough.

I moved out when I was 18. I was done dealing with my mother's strict rules. I packed a bag and was gone.

Some time later, I met this guy at a bar. Everything about him screamed "new immigrant". From the clothes he was wearing, to the fact that he barely spoke a word of English. He latched onto me and was determined to leave the bar with my number. But I knew better. I refused to give it to him. Three months later, I bumped into him at a Polish picnic. What were the chances of meeting him again in a big city like Toronto! When something like this happens, I become curious as to what life is telling me and I make sure to listen and learn. So I gave him a chance. We started talking and not only did I find him smart, but I liked the way we connected. I thought he was interesting. He bought me lunch and by the end of the evening I decided to give him my number. I thought, it wouldn't hurt to give my phone number to someone who sounded smart and interesting. Little did I know we would become life partners...

Despite some amazing moments, life has never been easy, which is why I believe in hard work.

When my husband and I got married, I was working a job I didn't really like and saw no real future in it. My life went something like this: I'd go to work and at the end of the day I would come home and watch TV. And so another day would go by.

One day, it dawned on me that this was not a true life that I was leading. I was simply existing; surviving. I was a dead person walking. I had to make some sort of change, because I was either going to drive myself crazy or worse, risk becoming suicidal.

In the midst of all this, we decided to start a family. The thought quickly obsessed me. But it just wasn't happening. I simply couldn't get pregnant. No matter how much we tried, even with the doctors' help, nothing worked; nothing happened.

It was frustrating having to do the same thing over and over again while expecting a miracle! I know this rule so very well.

I was committed to welcome in more change. So I decided to think differently. We adopted a dog and named him Buddy! But I was still lonely and unhappy.

It wasn't easy adapting to Buddy and I guess Buddy felt the same way too. I thought to myself: "what the hell was I thinking?" But I had already made a decision: he was part of our family. I was committed. Slowly I came to the realization that he brought a lot of happiness into my lonely life. He gave me a purpose and best of all, he gave me the ability to dream again. Buddy made me aware and alive. I started dreaming and believing in myself again.

Then, as if by magic, all the pieces of my life fell into place!

Three months after Buddy became part of our family, I found myself pregnant and soon welcomed our newborn son. I loved every minute of my new life. I felt blessed. It was time to start rediscovering myself!

I started asking myself what I loved and what I was passionate about. The answer came to me: My home! I was passionate about my home! I undertook making many improvements to it, embellishing it, letting my creativity run the way it wanted to, and I began to feel very good about it.

PEEKING BEHIND THE SCENES

In the process, I found myself pregnant again. What?! Was I ready? My doctor certainly didn't think so. In fact, she suggested an abortion. I had major complications birthing my first child and she had great concerns for this second pregnancy. I firmly said NO to her! This is my life, this is a life, it had a reason to be here, and I was not going to have it any other way!

I give birth to a healthy girl. I thought to myself: everyone told me that it was going to be impossible, that the scar from the previous C-section would burst and it would be a nightmare...
Yet, I took this as a sign to follow my heart and my dreams. If your heart and your mind are saying you can do something, don't believe in what others tell you. Listen to yourself; listen to your instincts.

When my daughter was 8 months old, I decided to put the house up for sale. My real estate agent told me I'd make money on it, but not a whole lot. You see, I had orange countertops in my kitchen that people would not like. In other words, it could be a deal breaker!
Needless to say, it was exactly the opposite! People loved the counter tops. They were amazed at my bold decision to deviate from the norm. My house sold without a glitch and was the highest priced sale in the area at the time. This proved

my point again: you don't have to listen to everything that people say. Follow your heart, be bold, follow your dreams and you will achieve the unachievable!

At the same time, my mom and my friends told me I had lost my mind. I was moving from a perfectly finished house to what even **I** would label a dump. I renovated it and soon, I was ready to do it all again: selling, moving, and then renovating.

This time I moved to a home that I had found on my own. I was unhappy with the choices my real estate agent was making at the time. We just had a different way of seeing things, and we had different visions. So I set out to find a house on my own. I knocked on doors. Yes, I was uncomfortable knocking on strangers' doors. I didn't care what people thought of me. I had a goal and I was ready to do whatever it took to get there. And sure enough, I made it happen.

It soon dawned on me that I was slowly materializing into a real estate agent of my own sort! There was nothing stopping me from getting my real estate license and actually start doing what I loved doing. Why not make it into my profession?

Some people told me I could not be successful, because the market was saturated with realtors. I believe I'm unique in what I do! Like everything else, I understand it's a process and it will take time. There is a learning curve that naturally comes with anything any of us undertake, and I am always ready and willing to grow. I realize that at the beginning I have to work harder than I have ever worked before. Because it's something I have never done and I am completely stepping out of my comfort zone. I am stepping out into the unknown and I am doing something I have never done.

But ultimately my efforts and determination paid off and a new chapter in my life began the day I obtained my 'Realtor' license.

That's what I do today: I find homes for my clients, for family members, for friends. I not only renovate for myself, but I can help others improve their home, give them suggestions, and if someone is ready to listen and follow my ideas and guidelines, I can make money for them too! Working together as one team. This is my passion!

I work with people without expectations. My main goal is to help them meet their needs, and everything else will just follow. It must be a win-win arrangement for both parties. This is what I have wanted to do all my life. It's something that gives me pleasure and satisfaction, and no matter how busy I am I'm never too busy and too tired to keep doing what I love, and make a difference in someone's life.

Today, I know myself better than ever. I know who I am and I know what I want. I work on myself and on my own growth every day. It cultivates and defines who I am. I'm a mom to my two precious children Kassie and Noah, and to my amazing dog Buddy. I am also the wife of a very loving husband, Tomasz. We are well off and we live our life by design, the way we have always envisioned it for ourselves.

I have well defined goals and dreams. I put together vision boards, and I make sure I have things lined up. I write down my long-term and short-term goals, because I know if I don't, I won't achieve them.
It doesn't matter if they change. Most likely they will, because as I grow I will continue to evolve and so will my thoughts and ideas. The thing to remember is that it's important to keep writing them down.

Don't be a sheep! Stand above the crowd and make your own path - the one that is unique to you. If you don't know what your path is yet, start with little things that you like and then keep building on them. Then slowly adjust to change. Change is never easy. Change is hard, because the more you know, the more you grow. Your own friends and family may abandon you, but it is important to stay focused and to never give up.
There will be a lot of things on the way that will affect your life in some way. So educate yourself, read, progress.

PEEKING BEHIND THE SCENES

My goal every single day is to meet two new people. Whether it's at the bank or when I'm walking the dog, whether I'm going to build a friendship or not, it doesn't matter. My focus remains the same. I am building something.

I'm committed to meet people that have similar interests and goals. People who believe in their dreams and goals and who are willing to learn from each other.

The only way to success in life is to get yourself to where you want to be, and to surround yourself with the right people. It could be friends, family or your partner. They are the ones you can count on to be with you every step of the way and give you that little nudge when things don't always go the way you want them to.

Have a coach, have a mentor that will hold you accountable for your actions, because it's not going to be easy. The road to success is long and can be lonely at times, but in the end it's totally worth it.

Believe in the goals you set for yourself. If you set yourself achievable goals, and believe in yourself, then you will get there. Success will be inevitable!

Life will always be full of obstacles that will come your way. There's always something that will jump in and cut you off or interrupt what you are doing._STAY FOCUSED AND NEVER GIVE UP ON YOUR DREAMS.

I always knew I wanted to be successful. I knew that I wanted to change lives. I knew I didn't just want to be Aldona, who sold real estate. At the end of the day, life is not about making money, BUT KNOWING WHAT TO DO WITH IT AND HOW TO USE IT TO CHANGE LIVES.

Opportunities are endless. Life offers you many open doors. It's always a matter of perspective and it's about picking the right door to walk through. The possibilities are everywhere. At the beginning and through it all there will be more downs than ups. The only person you need to stay true to is yourself. Love yourself and remember you can't love anyone else if you don't love who you are FIRST.

PEEKING BEHIND THE SCENES

Kedian Jimenez

Kedian Jimenez was raised in New York City where he graduated from Dowling College with a BS in Computer Science and Mathematics. He has worked for large financial companies such as RBC and currently Credit Suisse as a software engineer. He is also a real estate investor in New Jersey and New York. Kedian is networking with businesses and world leaders to build strong connections with young entrepreneurs and to help industries understand our future leaders. His mission is to tackle environmental problems and help shift the wealth distribution around the world by sharing knowledge.

Kedianjimenez.com
Kdnjimenez.com/media
Kdnestate.com

Chapter 18

Resetting My Settings

By Kedian Jimenez

Success is measured in many different ways. Some measure their success by how much money they have earned. However, the numbers that come after a dollar sign are not the only indicator of how much success someone has achieved. It is just one of the most visible ways of gauging. Success is something that is subjective, and therefore I share with you what success is to me.

I cherish freedom, happiness, and overall growth. If I am achieving these things, then I consider myself successful. I like to take a 30,000 feet bird's eye view of myself and evaluate whether all these values are aligned at any given time in my life.

There are many levels to success, and honestly there is no cap. There is an unlimited amount of levels, which can only be determined by you! By linking all the paths to success, you will notice a common thread.

For me, success started with my natural curiosity and my thirst for learning… and the day I discovered my Reset button.

At 26, I consider myself to be successful as I am light years ahead of where I thought I would have been by now, and I have achieved milestones that otherwise would have only been accomplished years later in my life. I currently hold a 9 to 5 job where I have reached a high rank in the space of 2-3 years, as opposed to its usual 8-10 year lapse. As I personally grow and expand at an exponential rate, I see that entrepreneurship is more my path than that of working for someone else. So I am easing into that independence slowly while shifting the scales appropriately. My parents are proud of me. Heck, I'm proud of me! That said, looking back, life could have turned out very differently for me.

I was born in Queens, New York and grew up in the Inwood neighborhood, in New York City. We were what I would consider the "upper poor" class. Like many, we struggled with bills and payments, living paycheck to paycheck. We did not starve and we never ended up on the streets; my parents made sure that never happened. But money was always a topic of argument between them. I knew then that I wanted to be more and do better. Growing up around poverty, I witnessed some of my childhood friends end up in jail. I always made sure to separate myself from that, because I always wanted to find a better way. I was looking for a life where I didn't have to look over my shoulder all the time. I was deliberate about walking away from negativity, and to this day I still separate myself from it.

My mother and father were a huge influence on me. I would not be who I am today without them.

My parents are both immigrants from the Dominican Republic. My dad has always had a lust for learning. Like me, he is also a curious person. I remember how he loved to watch the discovery channel and was always interested in how things were made and how they worked. Throughout my young years, my dad has often reminded me that I have bigger opportunities than he ever had. Both of my parents always told me to achieve more, to do better and be better. Even when I was reaching my peak, they would still push me in an encouraging way. They were an enormous part of my support system: they were crucial in me building my confidence and my belief in myself.

My entire family has this mentality of "Move forward and become better". It feels like a relay race where you have to be the one to go forward: 'we got you here, now it's your turn to take it further'. I have been blessed with a great family, and I have always felt that responsibility to carry on with the baton.

I recently found out from my mother that my grade three teacher had approached her years ago, with concerns over me having ADD. My mother never whispered a word of it to me till 2 years ago. Mom didn't believe it for a second and was not ready to put that label on me. The teacher told her I never paid attention, I was distracted, and I always kept talking to the other students. What it came down to is that I didn't really have an interest in most things we were learning. In English class, I would look out the window. In social studies, I focused my energy on finding ways to tell jokes. Yet when it came to math and science, I was there 120%, engaged and alert. In fact, it felt effortless to get 90s in those two subjects. Meanwhile, I struggled with every other subject, fighting my way to stay above the average.

It wasn't until my freshman year in college that I had an epiphany. I realized that my high school grades did not affect my college grades. As simple as that may sound, it was a complete game changer for me. It meant that all the "slacking off" I did in high school could now be forgotten and I could turn it all around! No labels, no expectations, just a brand new me. From then on, I became an A-B student and graduated with a 3.4 GPA. How did this happen? Simple. It was nothing more than a hard reset. Like when you go into the settings of your iPhone and click on the "reset all" button. The memory is clear, and it's running as smooth as ever.

PEEKING BEHIND THE SCENES

Yup, I had found the magic of my own personal reset button!

I understood that my past did not define me, that it only made me better, and that it built my character. It was incredible to me how a simple mind shift could have such a tremendous impact.

I now knew my own formula for success.

Success breeds success. It's a law! Once you know what success feels like you can keep repeating that pattern over and over again.

Since discovering this, I have pushed that button time and time again. And every single time I have pushed it I was able to reach a new level in my life. That button alone permanently removed my fear from taking that next step and added excitement to starting something new. Powerful!

As I move forward, I am applying these same principles to my professional life. Human potential is unlimited, including my own. I wont reach my peak under someone else's business, because working under a title and for a salary is restricting to me. I have been interested in self-growth since I was 14. It's always been tremendously important for me to be better today than I was yesterday.

Unlike most Millennials I know who believe there is a path set for them by others, whether it be their parents or peers, I find myself not wanting to live up to the societal status quo. If that were the case for me, I would not be operating from purpose and my spirit wouldn't respond well, feeling like I have just settled. With this reset button, I know I can start anew and be successful. I am confident about that.

As a computer science graduate, I love the idea of creation through technology. Right now I use my skills in my day job, as I like to call it, but my ideas that are tied to these skills are on a much broader worldwide scale. I have many passions, but for now, my entrepreneurship is centered on one of the three pillars of wealth: Real Estate. I am currently focusing on wholesaling and short-term rentals.

Truth be told, I never had the intention and foresight to get involved with Real Estate. If you had asked me a few years back if I was interested in getting into Real Estate, I would have probably said no. In my mind, it just simply never showed up as a possibility. I didn't know of any mentors in that area, and I didn't have access to large amounts of capital to even get started.

I was introduced to Real Estate Investing when I was at a business/self-development event that was giving intros and demos of courses in financial strategies that lead to financial freedom. One of the speakers mentioned that contrary to popular belief, Real Estate Investing did not mean you had to have $100K+ of liquidity in order to get started. Now he had my full attention! He said that it just took creative strategies and persistence to see success in this realm. I was of the belief that it always took money to make money, but here this strange yet charismatic speaker was saying that I could build a Real Estate business on sweat equity alone.

Now, I've always been interested in making anything work, especially if it has already been done before, so the idea appealed to me. It became real to me once I looked over at my sister, and I uttered the words "Hey, would you like to be in Real Estate?"

At first, I was looking at Real Estate as a creative means of reaching financial goals in general, and I thought it would be a good fit for my sister. After all, I was already tied up with some other ventures like my own 9 to 5 as well as network marketing. It caught me by surprise, but I quickly learned that small successes in Real Estate Investing can be very intoxicating -- in a 'high on life' kind of way. I've always taken a fondness to numbers and understanding the things around me, so when the two came together during the next couple of courses, I realized that I might enjoy this.

Once I started investing in Real Estate, it wasn't every day that I felt this good, far from it. Yet when things went bad, I stuck with it, and when things went well, I really enjoyed it. Real Estate is not a vehicle with a one-way street: it offers many different ways to get into the industry and into business for yourself. It's <u>one</u> of the pillars of wealth with a multitude of possible solutions that can fit any need.

There are many different strategies in Real Estate: there is wholesaling, rehabbing, buy-and-hold, lending and within those, there are niches and sub niches like residential, commercial, etc. There was a whole new world that presented itself to me, and I was ready to take it on.

I pressed the reset button of my mindset and off I went.

Real estate has introduced me to wonderful people, and there have been many advantages to it that other asset classes cannot compete with. Real Estate offers great tax incentives, because the government likes for investors to bring up the value and income of the city and state. Real Estate allows for financing, because a bank will loan you money based on a home, which is a hard asset, unlike a stock for example. Real Estate is also a necessity for people and contains several different commodities within a home that regardless if the dollar were to fall tomorrow, the house would still have some material and shelter value. Real Estate is also a class that has been proven to produce more millionaires than any other class. I'm loving what I am doing now. I love the creative aspect of it as well as the solution finding twist. It's all about making it possible and making it work.

I have been given many labels over the course of my young life. A label is how people associate you with something. It's the way each of us is perceived in the eyes of someone else. Now a label can be negative or positive. I've had both. Labels have really been part of my marketing piece. I just didn't know it. In fact, it's part of my brand. Many of my peers know me as a happy-go-lucky. Some even know me as the party guy. The last thing that was expected of me was to be in the realm of self-development. I realize I am very malleable. Lately, I keep hearing on the daily that I am different than what people remember of me. To me, that's my gauge of how fast I am morphing, growing and progressing. Self-development also leads to self-improvement, which is the most important key to advancement. It's about growing into the person you need to become.

My curiosity is what drives me the most. I keep finding ways of learning, and it helps me unravel the world. Right now, I'm not sure what my absolute end goal is in life. I have faith I will figure it out in due time. What I do know is that it has to do with taking humanity a step further in our process of evolving and adapting. Whether it's to help one person from their problems around life, or to help humans expand on to new worlds. Mars awaits!

I strongly believe that innovation and technology will consume most of the repetitive and labor intensive jobs and problems that we face today. Although that would mean a temporary decline in employment, it also does present a new opportunity, which is that now people will be focused on purpose-driven work. And that can never be accomplished by technology or without the human touch. Ultimately, if we can step away from focusing on minutia problems like paying bills or asking for a raise and if we can eliminate the financial trouble and other problems that are just level one issues, we can start focusing on the big problems that affect us as an entire specie. We can dedicate a larger amount of brainpower into taking on the important issues. Environment will improve. Wars will decline. People will be happier. Humans will grow.

Sometimes my goals and aspirations feel so elusive, but it is still something I see and can always get to. I take comfort in knowing that if I can see it all the way to the end, it means the vision is in fact too small.

At 26, I am by far not a millionaire or a billionaire. Yet I know I have time on my side. What I can be certain of is that I am better today than I was yesterday. At the moment, I am focusing on keeping my commitments, my biggest one being to utilize my reset button to do better and be better. Because I need to be the example I want to see in the world.

PEEKING BEHIND THE SCENES

Linda P. Cousineau

Linda P. Cousineau, CEO, *LPC and Associates Inc.* is a Canadian bilingual entrepreneur who has extensive consulting, coaching and training experience with clients in Europe and North America.

She has worked with industries such as: automotive, banking, brewery, Canadian forces, hospitals, legal, medical, mining, pharmaceutical, postal service, product manufacturing, retail, translation, travel, and more.

Linda helps organizations/individuals achieve results such as:
Create long-term personal/business relationships
Connect faster
Accelerate current sales revenue
Positively impact corporate culture, and more!

"She has a penetrating insight into what motivates and inspires individuals to achieve dynamic and permanent change in their performance and attitude."

www.LPCandassociates.com
https://www.linkedin.com/in/linda-p-cousineau-865a106a
linda@LPCandassociates.com

Chapter 19

A Life Long Journey...

By Linda P. Cousineau

When I was a little girl, I had all the stars at my disposal any time the sky was clear. It seemed so magical to me! I would seek out shooting stars just so I could have my wish granted. There were two things I constantly wished for as a child. One of them was: "Peace on Earth". Why? I'm not sure. I was only 4 years old. I just knew that was compelling to me. I was very thankful for my parents, my brother and my sisters. My life was wonderful and I wished for that peace and contentment for all the kids in the world. Somehow I felt not everyone was as lucky as I was. To this day, the same wish comes to mind when I hear: "make a wish".

I consider myself lucky to have grown up in the country, in a big French family with tons of cousins. Family values were very important, and we were all very close. I remember being shy and reserved, yet according to my mother, I was a quiet little leader and a natural coach. I had great admiration for nature. It was my best friend. During the day, when no one was looking, I would thank the birds for their beautiful melodies, the sun for its warmth, the trees for their energy...

The grown-ups' favorite activities were fishing and hunting. So in the fall, when they came back with their kill, I would have my own little ritual. Once everyone was back in the house, I would get in the box of the truck, stroke the animals' fur, and thank them for the meat they would provide. I would apologize for taking them away from their loved ones. Then I would ask *"Mother Nature"* to forgive us. Deer were especially beautiful. Moose had something very mysterious about them. They were so huge and looked so majestic! I had no idea at the time they would come to have a huge impact on my life!

Years later, I became a hunter too. I loved spending hours in my tree stand or sitting against a tree trunk, left with my thoughts and memories of previous years and friends gone by. Nature always had so much to offer. Once I spent an entire afternoon watching four little bears play for hours right under my tree stand. Another year, while sitting by a creek, I watched three otters play for an entire afternoon. It was as if the world was their playground! One day, as I was about to leave to get back to our tent on top of the mountain, I heard a noise. I sat down again in the middle of the swamp, my back to a tree. To my surprise, moose started communicating with each other. They were all around me. I sat there for another hour, in the dark, scared and yet amazed by the concert I was privileged to hear… For some odd reason, they never noticed I was there.

PEEKING BEHIND THE SCENES

In October 1994, I shot a moose. I remember being happy, because my parents and my husband were so incredibly proud of me. But I cried and cried and cried in silence for months. I can still see that beautiful animal in front of me, full of life. And then, gone!

Ironically, six months later, I was to meet what would become not only my biggest life challenge, but also my biggest life change.

It was a beautiful Sunday afternoon, May 28, 1995, to be exact. My two work colleagues and I were supposed to leave mid-afternoon and drive to a conference, which was starting the following day. The weather was so fantastic that we decided to spend more time with our respective families, leaving much later than previously planned. Little did I know, that decision would mark a significant turning point in my life.

By the time we left, the beautiful weather had turned into a very dark and misty night. It was not raining but almost. Around 11:00 pm, while driving across Algonquin Park in northern Ontario, our car collided with not one, not two, but three moose. I don't know how long it took me to gain consciousness. When I called for my colleagues, neither one of them answered. I assumed the worst. It took me a while to get the courage to push my door open and get out of the car. It was not a pretty sight! I will spare you the details…

That night was quite traumatic and completely surreal. Fortunately, both my colleagues regained consciousness eventually. They weren't looking good, but they were alive... That was enough for me to be happy.

Our phones did not work and it took a few hours before a car drove by. Eventually, the rangers and the ambulance arrived and we were taken to the closest hospital. My colleagues' injuries turned out to be surface wounds from the shattered windshield. I was the one that was the least hurt. Or at least so we thought... Once the hospital released us, we were driven to a near-by motel.

I slept for a few hours and woke up very early in the morning. I was so itchy. I got up and noticed my bed was covered in glass. I found out later, the pieces of glass had entered my skin during the impact of the accident and my body was now rejecting them...

Since I could not stop thinking about the previous night, I started walking down the road. The village was still asleep, so were my colleagues. It was very foggy and quiet. My heart skipped a beat and I screamed when a dog joined me for a few minutes. Then he disappeared into the fog. I walked without knowing where I was going. I wondered if I was actually dead and looking on from another world or if I was simply going to wake up from a really bad dream soon. I did not know what to think.

PEEKING BEHIND THE SCENES

In the middle of the afternoon, that same day, I couldn't feel my limbs. Later on, I found out I had deep tissue damage. Life as I knew it was about to change in a big way!

Never give up, even when tempted to!

In the weeks following the accident, I became consumed with physical and emotional pain. I could no longer enjoy the outdoors. Skiing, boating, canoeing, snowmobiling, gardening and all other activities I loved so much were no longer part of my life. I had to walk close to a wall as my balance was off. Being in a car was painful, as I could feel every little bump or pebble in the road. At one point, nights became days and days became nights... I was in pain from head to toe. My skin complexion was as white as a ghost. The worst of it all was the pain in my head, I felt like something was exploding. A few times, I found myself wishing I would die so the pain would go away... I could literally feel the very tiny layer of muscles that cover my head. I had suffered from migraines as a child and thought nothing could be worse. This pain made migraines feel like nothing. There were times, where I actually wondered how I could end it all. *I gained a different respect for suicide victims! If only they waited a bit longer, their despair may be replaced by a glimpse of hope, somehow!*

My road to healing was going to be a prolonged one. Physically, I wasn't the same person anymore. My bubbliness,

238

never ending energy, and "joie de vivre" were gone. I was reduced to sleeping most of the time and watched life go by. That was extremely difficult to accept!

Find something to believe in…

Yet, on better days, part of me kept thinking this was part of a bigger plan. Something was expected of me in this lifetime. I strongly believe things happen for a reason. Nothing happens for nothing. One day, I would understand why I survived the accident and had gone through such pain. I believed the answers would all be revealed to me in due time.
That belief kept me going and hoping! I just had to keep reminding myself to be patient.
Yes, patience tried me!

After a few years of living in pain, I left the corporate world. It was an environment that didn't suit me anymore. I remember being told by a top executive: *"You have been sick long enough, you should be fine by now"*. That day I realized most people do not believe what they can't see. Muscle pain related conditions (acute whiplash, post-traumatic stress disorder, myofascial restrictions, joint dysfunctions, etc.) were not well understood over 20 years ago. I had reached the point where I felt worthless and had nothing to offer. I needed to regain my self-confidence and self-worth. I needed to find a way to believe in myself again. It would take me years to get there.

PEEKING BEHIND THE SCENES

Perspective – be aware how you choose to look at situations

Because I had hunted before, most people automatically assumed I would want to get even and kill as many moose as I could. That was shocking to me. The three moose did not take my life, but lost theirs. I promised myself I would never hunt again. Our car collided with them while they were coming on the road to lick the salt on the pavement, just like a child enjoys a great ice cream! These poor animals were not to blame for my misfortune! What if I needed to go through all this to become the person I was to be?

Today, I am extremely thankful for the life and the many experiences I had prior to my accident. I am also extremely grateful to still be here! Experiencing emotional and physical pain made me, over time, the perfect confidant for those in pain. People often say: "I know how you feel", but if they have never gone through pain they simply can't understand.

I continued working in the skills development industry; it became a passion of mine. I met so many wonderful people whom, after the training sessions, would ask for a bit of my time privately. They simply wanted to release what they were holding inside without any inhibition, because they knew their secrets were safe with me. I had a purpose again!
What would have happened to me, to my soul if I had chosen to be angry and to get even? Where would I be now?

Find what you are passionate about

I started thinking I survived the accident so I could be of service to others… Right around that time, I found out about an amazing Coaching Program. I signed up. We learned the art of questioning to help people find their own answers. I was fascinated by the process. A Coach does not tell you what to do, a Coach asks you questions so you can discover what is important to you at the deepest of your core.

We all have the answers to our questions, we just need to allow and trust ourselves… This was easy for me, it made sense. We were also asked to write a personal declaration and vision. My vision came to me instantly in three words: "Free to Be". As I said it out loud, I was overwhelmed with emotion. Something had shifted.

Nine years later this statement still greatly resonates with me. I was now passionate about two things: skills development (training) and coaching.

Recently, I discovered a communication based proven methodology, which I embraced instinctively. It brought me back to the little girl I once was, the one who wished for "Peace on Earth". The genius behind this system is in its simplicity. It can be learned and applied immediately.

PEEKING BEHIND THE SCENES

In a small way, I help create a better world by training and coaching people in organizations to work together effectively while expanding their communicating skills and respect for each other. I support individuals and family members in their quest to communicate and appreciate each other's differences. It is very rewarding!

What if everyone simply wanted to be heard? What if everyone knew what to listen for? Could we minimize misunderstandings, frustration, arguments, and hatred? Could all children finally be allowed to be children? What if this was the tool required to change the world and make it a beautiful place for all…? I can't help but wonder!

Be patient, the answers will eventually come

A few months ago, I was asked to join a group of like-minded individuals to collaborate towards a Global Peace Initiative, which includes 196 nations. I met the most amazing people, all interested in making a positive difference in the world by increasing the level of peace, love and prosperity.
Again, I could not help but think of my childhood wish…

Shortly after, I was asked to write this chapter.

I have learned that life works in mysterious ways.

I accepted the invitation to write this chapter for different reasons:

Those of you in pain, I hope my story offers you hope!
Those of you hoping for a better life for everyone on this planet, know that different nations are working together to do just that! You can get involved…
Those of you wanting to expand your communication skills in order to connect at a deeper level with those around you, I am happy to share what I found out.
Those of you ready for the next step in your professional or personal life, that step is yours to take! Trust yourself!

It is interesting for me to look back and think of the journey I have had to travel in order to get to where I am now. I was once very discouraged and scared about the future. Now I am curious, excited, and energized by the possibilities again.

On the night of the Strawberry Moon (June 2016), I looked up at it in awe. I was taken back to the time when I was a child, when I was grateful for my life, and remembered how much I wished for "Peace on Earth". My vision statement "Free to Be" came back to me in a flash and it made me realize that it was always there. Helping people was always woven into who I am, since the very beginning! Hence my passion for Skills Development (training) and Coaching.

PEEKING BEHIND THE SCENES

I don't know yet what the rest of my story will be.

I am coming to the realization slowly but surely that my life purpose was already pre-determined to be big picture. And big picture does not happen over a decade or two. Big picture happens over a lifetime!
My life's goal is to make a difference in this world...

What's your big picture?

Al Hillman

AL Hillman grew up as a Navy kid and has lived all over the world. Al attended the University of Tennessee and Tennessee Temple University in Chattanooga TN. He currently lives in Winter Haven, Florida, with his family and is very active at Hillman Motors, Center State Leasing and ALH Real estate LLC. When he is not working, Al enjoys flying, boating and the Florida lifestyle.

Al can be reached at Autodealer@aol.com or thru his company web site at www.hillmanmotors.net

Chapter 20

Always Stretching and Always Striving

By Al Hillman

"You will never be successful. Go work for someone else". Well, I had bigger plans... It's been almost 28 years since I heard those words. I believe those same words are a big part of what made my business work so successfully all these years.

It was 1989. I had worked for several other car dealerships in the area, and I had learned the business inside and out. As a young man, I had paid my way through college by buying cars, fixing them and then reselling them. I knew my way around cars, and I knew I had a fail-safe plan. I was setting it up properly, right from the beginning. Networking was also a very important element of success to me, and I made it a point to always know the 'who's who'. I made sure to pay attention to who the biggest influencers were to me: all the bankers and people in my area that could help me succeed. I knew at some point I wanted to work for myself and own my own business. So my quest began. How was I going to get up and running with no money and just a dream?

Compiled by **JENNIFER LOW**

Here's what I did!

Paying attention to the economic climate can make you spot opportunities quite easily. In 1989, one such opportunity presented itself beautifully to me! The local Savings and Loans businesses were in trouble and were dumping foreclosed properties to anyone who had good credit and would take over the payments on the bad loans. So I stepped in and took over a few loans, not knowing how I would pay for them at the time. I knew I had to rent the properties to make the payments, so I worked day and night fixing them up and got them rented. I knew nothing about real estate and fixing up houses back then, but I read books and figured it out. Later I sold these properties for a profit and used that money to start Hillman Motors, Inc.

Once I got the doors open, I had to find more money to buy inventory. I went to every bank in town, and every single one turned me down one after another. I wasn't giving up. I was committed to my plan. Eventually, I found someone who was willing. The finance company TranSouth agreed to give me a $75,000 line of credit for one year. I used that money to strictly buy inventory. I bought the cars to put on my lot. I was bringing in a profit month after month. The only discrepancy was in my third month of business. Hillman Motors Inc. had started selling cars at the tail end of 1990, and at the beginning of 1991, the Gulf War broke out and seemed to have curtailed many businesses. Other than that month, the entire year was productive, and I made a profit in my first year. I put all that money back into the business.

I have been asked several times: "How did you make it your first year?" as many new start-ups go belly up in the first year. The key for me was again to know the who's who! Knowing who my true support team was, was vital to my business survival. I needed to know all the bankers that bought car loans in my area. I knew who would buy the loans or as we say in the car business "the paper". Placing that paper is the key to success in this business. And that came from working in the area and knowing the right people. You have to educate yourself in the business you want to go into. It's imperative. I knew this, so I made sure I kept learning and growing; plus I was well liked and had a great reputation in the area.

Once I was up and running and I knew the business was stable, my next step was to grow in order to make enough money to have the life and the lifestyle I was looking for. I wanted to be financially independent, have the ability and the means to travel, as well as come and go as I pleased. My lifestyle choice was that of ultimate freedom. I made it a point to hire the best people I could find and pay them well so they could be happy, committed, and work hard for my company. Many times they made more money than I did, but I could see the big picture. I knew that if I found the right combination of people for my task force, and worked that every day, I would see the growth and sales gains I needed in order to achieve the personal goals I had set for myself and for my business. And that's exactly what I did. I stuck to the plan and let the plan take me to where I needed to be!

In any business, you will need to modify the plan as things change around you, which is also what I did. I had to always keep my eyes open, keep my finger on the pulse of the economic climate, so I was always prepared for a quick shift if necessary, and embrace the changes in my field and in my market. When things change, you either change with them or die. Like the branch of a tree, we need to remain flexible to our time and our industry, otherwise, we risk getting snapped off. It needs to work like a dance. We change our rhythm with the industry, as we need to.

A lot has changed in my business and industry over the last 28 years. We flow with it, and we adapt. Yet some things will always remain the same: the desire for success, hard work, and dedication, and the constant influx of questions: "How bad do you want it? How many negative people are you going to let influence you? Do you have a vision and a plan to get you there?" I wanted it, and I stuck to the plan. Several million dollars later, I am glad I went for it, and never lost the focus and the dream.

PEEKING BEHIND THE SCENES

It was not an easy road, and there were times when I just wanted to quit. I had times where I would go home at night still thinking about the day and what I could have done better. What I learned from all the nights where I went to bed reliving that day that had just gone by, was that it was really about looking at what worked and what didn't work, and applying what I had learned from the daily experiences in business. It was key to me to keep my desire to win in front of me all the time. I always wanted to be my own boss and live life on my terms, so I just kept going, learning and growing.

My business also lived through some very lean years. During the housing debacle when the economy tanked in 2008-2009, all the banks became very tight as far as their lending practices went. This meant that our sales volume went down, because of the inability of being able to put people in loans. Many a times, my employees got paid and I didn't. I was adamant about holding on to a good team, so I rearranged it from the inside and made it work, despite the insecurity of the unknown timeframe.

One of my big dreams back then was also to be a pilot and own my own jet and fly my family to different places. I posted a picture of a Citation Jet on my computer, on my mirror in my bathroom, and at the office. Seeing that goal in front of me all the time kept me on track.

It may not be a Jet for you; it might be something else. Your big dream may be a big bank account, a house or a trip, or to do something special for someone else. We are all different and different things motivate us. Find your motivation and put it before you every day, and never lose sight of it. It can be a thing, a relationship or even an achievement in your education. Whatever that goal and that desire of yours is, keep it in front of you. You should never be satisfied, but rather always have something you are stretching and striving for. That is the fuel that will keep you going in good and in hard times. Once you have achieved your desired goal, put a new one in front of you.

I have since earned my pilot's license, have over 1000 hours as pilot in command and have owned four prop planes over my lifetime. Flying is still a big part of my life, despite still being currently very involved in multiple businesses. I have several rental properties as well as my car business. I'm still working on the Jet, and I'm sure one day soon I will own one. I still have that picture in front of me every day. Yes 28 years later I still see the picture of the Jet on my computer and mirror, and it's just a matter of time till I achieve that goal.

As I look back over the last 28 years, I see a young man of 28 years of age, working hard to do whatever it took to achieve the goals I had set for myself and to become a success. Now at 55, I see the results of all the hard work and effort that went into this dream. I see the different benchmarks that were reached along the way. I see my kids now with their goals, following in my footsteps in obtaining their dreams. I see a business that is 28 years old with a name that everyone in town knows and respects. I see all the trappings that a successful business can help afford: homes, vacations and all the things that make life fun and exciting. I see good health, in body and spirit. I see a man in the mirror that was told time and time again that he couldn't do it. I was told to give up the dream and find a real job.

With God's help, a solid vision, and a resolve to succeed, I see the results, and I'm happy to say, I didn't take their advice, I didn't give up, and it paid off. In fact, it paid off in a huge way. I would have rather failed than never tried. Most importantly I see a man who's dreams and hard work were truly blessed, and I am so thankful for all the people who invested their time with me, who believed in me, and who helped me get to where I am today.

Tomorrow is a new day, and as I am writing this, we are in negotiations with a major boat company with the intention of expanding Hillman Motors Inc. We may be selling new boats in the near future. Boating has always been a favorite pastime of mine, and I have always owned a boat. In my younger years, I would waterski on the local lakes. So it was a natural thing to transition into, especially here in Florida. Again, my objective is to create a plan to sell boats in my market area, find my niche and stick to the plan.

Success starts with you. If you want to be successful, you have to do the things successful people do. Educate yourself and most importantly never give up. It's really not rocket science!

PEEKING BEHIND THE SCENES

Sandi Cohen P.S.

Sandi is fiercely committed to guiding others to achieve financial and spiritual success as well as P.O.M. This is Peace of Mind so others can Live Life As It Should Be!

She personally mentored dozens of million dollar earners.
She has been an AGELESS ADVOCATE for over 20 years, empowering people who want to live longer, and healthier so they can thrive as they age and lead by example.

She is a Co-Founder and Board member of the ANMP (Association of Network Marketing Professionals) and featured in Amazon best sellers, and several other publications.

Every tomorrow is a vision of Hope.

P (702) 381.3799
www.SandiandEd.com
www.Facebook.com/Sandi.Cohen2

PEEKING BEHIND THE SCENES

Chapter 21

Confessions of an Overnight Success

By Sandi Cohen P.S.

Imagine turning 52 years old, being $450,000 in debt, and losing everything you've ever had. I thought I was set for the rest of my life and never thought this could happen to me.

GONE: 10,000 square foot home, every room elegantly furnished, a Rolls Royce, a Stretch limo, a Corvette, and a staff including an English houseman, a cook from Grand Cayman, and summers in the South of France. Yes, all gone!

How in the world did this happen, you may ask?

Ed and I met when I was 15 years old. I had braces on my teeth... Ed often says, that when we met, there was a glow about me, then he realized it was the light reflecting from my braces. LOL.

We both graduated from Temple University, myself with a BS in Education and Ed with a degree in Pharmacy. In 1963, I volunteered to be the first white female in an all black school in North Philadelphia. One of my passions was to make a difference.

Over a short period of time, Ed had 5 Pharmacies along with all the burden that is entailed with traditional businesses.

In life, I have found things often happen without intentional planning.

Due to a series of circumstances when clients of our pharmacies could not get necessary medical supplies because other providers would not accept "assignment", I felt compassion for their struggle and volunteered to provide the service.

In 1978, I began to build my medical and surgical supply business. Whenever a patient, physician, or hospital needed something that they could not acquire or had to have third party insurance billed, I provided the service and then waited to be paid. This payment process often took 60-90 days or more... a very cash intensive business.

Within 3 years, we had a multi-million-dollar business servicing Pennsylvania, New Jersey and Delaware. I loved making a positive difference in the lives of those who had health challenges and often, moms who were left alone to care for a child with special needs.

PEEKING BEHIND THE SCENES

Achieving success came with enormous burden: 36 employees, overhead, accounts payables, millions of dollars in receivables, half a million in inventory, and 6 trucks delivering equipment and supplies.

Fast forward to 1986. Healthcare was changing. Medicare was not paying. They gave excuses of "new computer software" issues... but our employees did not care. We were left with no cash flow. Ed and I took no salary, but our employees had to be paid every Friday.

We then decided to sell the business. We sold it to a group of private investors, and within several months, they defaulted and did not pay us.

So began our nightmare in the court system in Philadelphia. Eight years later, we were finally getting our day in court, but the company had gone out of business about six months after the litigation had started.

When the Judge stood up, he threw a stack of books on the floor of the courtroom and shouted, "Counsel, in my chambers. Now!" We had no idea what was going on. The judge was so angry with the group of men who had harmed us that he forced them to settle without a costly jury trial.

That was the good news.

The bad news was that the settlement was small. After the attorney's got their "piece", we were dead right, dead broke, and $450,000 in debt.

During this period of our eight-year nightmare, I had said to Ed: "If I have to start my life over at the age of 52, I want to see sunshine every day!" And we moved West to Arizona.

After having lived the lifestyle of the rich and famous, we now moved into a small townhouse and shared a 9-year-old car with no air-conditioning. It was particularly challenging in the summer when it was 110 degrees Fahrenheit in the shade and roll-up windows that didn't work.

You know what happens before it gets better, don't you? Yes, it gets progressively worse once you find yourself in a "downward spiral".

A friend gifted me Dr. M. Scott Peck's book, *The Road Less Travelled*. The first 3 words in the first chapter were LIFE IS DIFFICULT. And Dr. Peck goes on to explain that as life's challenges try to stop your progress, you need to find a way around them, over them, through them, but not to let your dreams die within you.

PEEKING BEHIND THE SCENES

Obstacles. Challenges. I would go to bed crying. I would wake up crying. And things got even worse.

My mother was taken ill with breast cancer and Alzheimer's. There was no way I was going to put my mother in a nursing home, so we brought her to live with us in Arizona, to be diapered, tube fed, and on oxygen 24/7. There were times where we couldn't pay both the electric bill and the phone bill. The only reason the electricity didn't get shut off, was because Mom was on oxygen for her life support.

During those early days in Arizona, someone introduced me to a woman who re-introduced me to Network Marketing. Years before, I had convinced Ed to purchase $8,000 in water filters that had to be given to Goodwill when we couldn't sell them at any price. That's when I promised him that I would never ever approach the subject of Multi Level Marketing again. But, I kept hearing her words: "if you are willing to help others, you might get your life back."
I was not going to allow that one bad experience in Network Marketing stop me from achieving my ultimate goals.

Did you ever try to do something and no matter how hard you tried, it did not work?
I saw people making some outrageous incomes.
What did they know and do, that I did not know and do?

As Ed kept pushing me to go get a JOB, I told him boldly: "I will figure this out!' Working for someone else will never get us out of debt. And you working as a Pharmacist for others will not either. And when I do figure it out, I will help others shortcut their success so they can achieve their goals."

I had blind faith and believed that I would attain success.
It only took me five years, full time, to become an overnight success.

I understood the Pareto Principal… the 80/20 rule.
I researched and found that the majority of success in almost any profession comes from only about 20% of those who are driven to success.

You may ask yourself how does a Network Marketing business compare to any other profession or traditional business?

Look at realtors, insurance agents, physicians, business people… it's not the 80% that experience true success, but only 20%. I was determined to be a part of that 20%.

According to the U.S. Bureau of Labor Statistics, there were 157,660 real estate agents in the United States in 2014. The National Association of REALTORS®' total membership for October 2016 month end was 1,235,827.

PEEKING BEHIND THE SCENES

According to the BLS, real estate agents earned a median salary of $40,990 in 2014. The best paid earned about $105,270, while the lowest-paid earned approximately $21,540.

According to a report on food franchising by Franchise Business Review, 51.5 percent of food franchises earn profits of less than $50,000 a year; roughly 7 percent top $250,000, with the average profit for all restaurants coming in at $82,033. That doesn't sound too bad until you factor in the initial investment.

The myth that franchises are less prone to failure than other small businesses is simply that: a myth! The reality is that they generally go out of business at the same rate. However, which franchise you choose can make a big difference, says Kelly, who was interviewed. Some franchise chains have failure rates as high as 80% to 90%.

Those who commit to the journey can, and will succeed at varying levels, but the numbers of the Pareto's Principle will also apply. Not everyone will do what the 20% who succeed are willing to do.

Knowing Pareto's Principle should serve as a daily reminder to focus 80 percent of your time and energy on the 20 percent of the work that is really important to you. Don't just "work smart", work smart on the right things!

Of the things you do during your day, only 20 percent really matter. Those 20 percent produce 80 percent of your results. Identify what those things are and focus exclusively on them. When the fire drills of the day begin to sap your time, remind yourself of the 20 percent you need to focus on. If something in the schedule has to slip, if something isn't going to get done, make sure it's not part of that 20 percent.

If you can figure out which 20% of your time produces 80% of your business results, you can spend more time on those activities and move forward in your business success.

As I reflect on the early days of my struggle, I met another woman who introduced me to Esther Hicks and the teachings of Abraham. At first, I was reluctant, thinking it was some "religious cult". But being open minded, I found that the teachings were already something I believed in… In fact, I adopted the saying **"You are where your thoughts are. Make sure your thoughts are where you want to be!"**

It was not easy, but we were committed to do whatever we could to find positive thoughts and feelings to help us on our journey back to living life, as it should be: with joy, love, abundance and the prosperity promise.

Daily I would listen to positive audios and read books while developing my personal and professional skills to what successful people do and say…

PEEKING BEHIND THE SCENES

I put pen to paper and INKED my daily, weekly and monthly goals.

And guess what? We attracted positive things to us.

We found, "Not only does the thought you are choosing right now attract the next thought and the next . . . and so on — it also provides the basis of your alignment with your *Inner Being*. As you consistently and deliberately think and speak more of what you *do* want and less of what you *do not* want, you will find yourself more often in alignment with the pure, positive essence of your own Source; and under those conditions, your life will be extremely pleasing to you." (Abraham)

In fact, to inspire and empower others, we now have our own website where we share many of the tools that assisted us in helping others as well as ourselves.

Please visit www.SandiandEd.com and embrace the magic of you achieving what you desire so that you too can live the life you want to live and not settle.

One of the books featured on our site is *Ask and it is Given*, by Esther and Jerry Hicks. The principals and exercises Abraham teaches helped us overcome enormous obstacles.

We are so pleased to share our story of HOPE and what is possible with hard work and determination.

For us, Network Marketing became the vehicle to achieve success, because we were willing to invest in others. We have helped dozens earn a million dollars or more, but most importantly, we have helped tens of thousands earn thousands.

We are now at a new crossroad and starting our second wave of success stories.

Network Marketing is a team effort... unlike traditional businesses with enormous financial risk. The investment is in your own personal and professional growth.

Finding a mentor that can shortcut your success is an obvious fast track solution.

Network Marketing is not for everyone.
Often the extraordinary products you can purchase at a discount are a good reason to join a company. If people understood the HUGE Tax Advantages of a home based business everyone would want to set aside, legally, $300-$500 a month. All that is required is to work at your part-time, home based business for a minimum of 7-10 hours a week.

PEEKING BEHIND THE SCENES

No matter what your profession or career of choice, you should always strive to be the best you can be at whatever you do.

Make a decision to begin doing what you love doing.

NOW is the time to put your foot on the gas and go for what you really want.

"The only limit to our realization of tomorrow will be our doubts of today."
-Franklin D. Roosevelt

Let me leave you with a little story:

Lessons From a Carrot, an Egg, and a Coffee Bean

"Let's face it. Painful personal trauma and tragedy – like illness or injury, death of a loved one, loss of a job, or an unexpected breakup of a relationship – are unavoidable.

The question is: Will these private calamities erode our capacity to be happy or cause us to become stronger and better able to live a meaningful and fulfilling life?

Consider how differently carrots, eggs, and ground coffee beans are affected by the extreme adversity of being boiled.

266

Like a carrot, adversity can soften us. We can emerge more flexible, understanding, compassionate, and grateful, or we can let our life spirit turn into a soft mush.

Like an egg, boiling water can make us harder, stronger, tougher, and wiser, or we can become more cynical, pessimistic, callous, and inaccessible.

And like a coffee bean, we can willingly transform our lives into something better or lose ourselves completely.

We can't control what happens to us, but we have a lot to say about how we react and, therefore, what happens in us. The first step to turning adversity into an advantage is to get out of the hot water as quickly as possible. Don't dwell on catastrophe. Grieve, but move on. Don't define your life by misfortune.

Second, force yourself to move forward. Draw on your inner strengths, the people who love you, and your faith to transform your life into something better. Formulate a vision of a more purposeful life filled with people and experiences that will help you become more fulfilled." Michael Josephson

Think about what you want.
And don't let anyone or anything stop you from achieving it.

PEEKING BEHIND THE SCENES

Conclusion

Twenty one amazing stories of challenges and obstacles never too big to overcome. Stories of inspiration, of beating the odds, of going for what you believe in. Many different stories with the same skeleton: an event, a decision, a determination, perseverance, consistency, discovery, growth, and through it all, triumph and pride.

Each one of us has our own mountain to climb.

I know each one of these authors has provided you with many tools for you to start your journey. There are nuggets in each one of these chapters and treasures from each person's life experience.

Please remember along your way, that an uphill climb (a turn around) does not happen overnight. It takes time to power back up and to find that momentum working in your favour. Sometimes it can be months, sometimes it can be years.

Patience!

To establish any sort of momentum, it will require you to be consistent and persistent. You cannot let go of what is driving you. Lock on to it and keep doing the activity and the work towards what you want to achieve, no matter what happens or how many distractions appear on your path. Focus is imperative!

Find out what you love and then do it with passion. Sometimes, that will be the only fuel (or fumes) that will keep you moving past the pain and potential fear.

Growth is absolutely essential to your climb. Longer legs will help you get to the top of your mountain quicker. Success always starts with the self. It's about developing strong personal, professional and mental skills. Grow yourself into the person you want to become!

Make a decision! Choosing one is critical.
Write it down so as to magnify it.
Finally, be responsible about your commitment.
Your success depends on what you become!

I invite you to get in contact with any of these authors to guide you and mentor you on your climb.

Please share your success story with me by emailing me at jennifer@peekingbehindthescenes.com

Have a happy journey. I will see you at the top.

*   *   *

Compiled by **JENNIFER LOW**

PEEKING BEHIND THE SCENES

When you start to polish any area of your life, you can watch it transform before your eyes. Now imagine that transformation with a ripple effect... How much could your life grow by adding that polish?

If you are open to expanding your life, go to www.anauthenticu.com/schedule/ and book your free 30 min consultation with me. Let's talk about possibilities.

Do you have a book inside of you that has been lying dormant for years? It's about time you let it out. I would love to pull it out of you and help you put it on paper once and for all. To know more about this process, contact me at Jennifer@anauthenticu.com

THE END